Praise for

Model Mormon

"Rosie and her story are multidimensional, complicated, and marvelous. In her jaunty prose, Rosie bravely exposes her fears, insecurities, and regrets alongside her faithful testimony, life lessons, and inspiration. In doing so, she encourages each of us to remake our vision of the 'ideal Mormon life' into one that more closely resembles the reality in which we each live. This book is raw, real, and resonant."

—Eva M. Witesman, BYU professor and
opinion columnist for the *Deseret News*

"Not only did Rosemary manage to write a super engaging story but she also packed it full of powerful lessons and profound insights from her experiences as an international supermodel who fought hard to remain the 'good little Mormon girl' her parents raised her to be. This book is an important read for members of the rising generation who are trying to figure out a way to live a Christ-centered life in a world that's anything but Christ-centered. It's also for all those who have felt alone in the world or maybe even like an outcast just for being different from their peers. And lastly, this book is really for anyone who is looking for a fun and easy read that will simultaneously broaden their perspective on life and deepen their testimony of being a beloved child of heavenly parentage."

—Kristyn and Greg Trimble, authors of
Moms Who Stay and Fight and *Dads Who Stay and Fight*

"I hope every member of the Church (from leaders to our younger members) will read Rosemary Card's new book. Thank you for sharing your courageous story. It outlines Christlike principals for making great decisions and successfully navigating the complex issues in our restored Church. It gives vision to our women and how they can grow, develop, and use all their talents for good in the world. Reading it has increased my faith in the Church and my confidence in our younger members. They are the best of the best."

—Richard "Papa" Ostler, married father of six children, former YSA bishop, believer in our younger members

"A perfect read for angst. Rosie's unfettered words and her approach to real life are refreshing and hopeful."

—Tamara Uzelac Hall, editor, speaker for BYU Women's Conference and Temple Square Youth Conferences, and former seminary and institute teacher

"*Model Mormon* is an endlessly interesting and deeply beautiful, funny, inspiring, and sometimes challenging book. It's also a firm testament to the importance of women's stories and women's voices, including Mormon women's stories and Mormon women's voices. Please read this book."

—Rachel Hunt Steenblik, author of *Mother's Milk: Poems in Search of Heavenly Mother*

Model Mormon

FIGHTING FOR SELF-WORTH ON THE RUNWAY AND AS AN INDEPENDENT WOMAN

ROSEMARY CARD

CFI
An imprint of Cedar Fort, Inc.
Springville, Utah

ISBN 13: 978-1-4621-2208-0

Published by CFI, an imprint of Cedar Fort, Inc.
2373 W. 700 S., Springville, UT 84663
Distributed by Cedar Fort, Inc., www.cedarfort.com

LIBRARY OF CONGRESS CATALOGING-IN-PUBLICATION DATA

Names: Card, Rosemary, 1989- author.
Title: Model Mormon : fighting for self-worth on the runway and as an
   independent woman / Rosemary Card.
Description: Springville, Utah : CFI, an imprint of Cedar Fort, Inc., [2018]
   | Includes bibliographical references and index.
Identifiers: LCCN 2018004622 (print) | LCCN 2018007072 (ebook) | ISBN
   9781462129034 (epub, pdf, mobi) | ISBN 9781462122080 (perfect bound : alk.
   paper)
Subjects: LCSH: Card, Rosemary, 1989- | Mormon women--Biography. | Child
   models--Biography. | LCGFT: Autobiographies.
Classification: LCC BX8695.C2735 (ebook) | LCC BX8695.C2735 A3 2018 (print) |
   DDC 289.3092 [B] --dc23
LC record available at https://lccn.loc.gov/2018004622

Cover design by Martha Christensen
Cover design © 2018 Cedar Fort, Inc.
Edited and typeset by Kathryn Watkins and Kaitlin Barwick

Printed in the United States of America

10 9 8 7 6 5 4 3 2 1

Printed on acid-free paper

For Judy Strain.
I'll never let moss grow under my feet.

And Ted.

Contents

I'm Rosie, as Seen on Mutual

Okay, before we get started, I need to get something off my chest. I'm not Obama and I know it. Anyone who has seen my Tinder, Bumble, or Mutual accounts (I swipe in faith) knows I'm a pretty standard twenty-nine-year-old woman. I stay up to date in politics, love Arby's, drive a beat-up Subaru, and routinely casually brag about how long it's been since I last washed my hair. I haven't changed the course of history (yet) or accomplished any kind of athletic feat, nor have I done anything that would win me any medals. I burn quesadillas on the regular.

I'm starting off with a super convincing argument to get you to keep reading, aren't I? Early on in the process of writing this book, I thought to myself, *Oh my gosh. Why would anyone care?! I'm a twenty-nine-year-old who still applies her eyeshadow with her fingers and has never spelled* entrepreneur *right the first try. People are going to think I think they care!* Like I said: I'm no Obama. But that's okay because Obama is Obama and I'm Rosemary Card.

Though I am just shy of clocking three decades on earth, I have stories to share. I recognize that it is a rare opportunity to write and publish my life story in such a so-far-so-good manner. I am grateful for the opportunity I have been given, and unlike most people who say that before a lesson or a talk, I sincerely mean it.

I also recognize how especially unique of an opportunity it is to share my story as a woman. Not too many years ago, women's stories were considered unimportant. Our stories were deemed so unimportant that we were only mentioned in passing if we were someone's wife, daughter, or temptress/mistress/princess or any other -esses. I feel deeply blessed to live in a time where women's stories are valued and believed. I look forward to the day that this statement rings even truer. I get pumped thinking about more and more people, women and men, recognizing and valuing women's stories and those stories being told in their own words.

So this is my story, in my own flawed and developing words. My story matters simply because all stories matter. Especially the ones with puppies in them. If my story matters, yours sure as heck does too.

In my adulthood, realistically the last four years, I have tried to never shy away from sharing my thoughts. I tend to feel pretty comfortable sharing my opinions over the family dinner table, on most first dates, and especially with the general public via the wonderful world of social media. Now, I know, I know. "I read a Facebook post that completely opened my eyes and mind to the opposing side, and I've changed my position," said no one ever. I just can't help it.

In her TED Talk "Your Elusive Creative Genius," Elizabeth Gilbert shares the creative experience of various writers. Mainly, she addresses how ideas come to specific individuals and how those ideas turn into something more tangible. Ruth Stone, an American poet, explains that when she would be out working in the field, she could sense a poem "like a thunderous train of air . . . barreling down at her over the landscape. . . . And she would run . . . to the house and she would be getting chased by this poem, and the whole deal was that she had to get to a piece of paper and a pencil fast enough so that when it thundered through her, she could collect it and grab it on the page."[1] If you've ever had an idea that felt important, you know you rarely have a say when and how those ideas come.

For me, ideas typically come when I'm in the car, having a good conversation with someone I respect, or while watching a good movie. Rarely do they come when I'm in a situation conducive to writing and pondering. When it comes to creative ideas, I can sort most of my own into two categories. The first saunters into my mind, floats around for a bit, nods to its acquaintances, but if I'm not in a place to act on that idea, if I can't presently welcome it into my life with open arms, it floats away to who I imagine is someone readier to receive it. Then there is the second type of idea. These ideas don't invite me to act upon them if I'm interested. These ideas kick in the front door and smash through the windows SWAT style. These ideas enter my mind armed and dangerous, and they've already called for reinforcements. They're quickly running the show, and they take no prisoners. In that moment, they commandeer all other thought paths and things that feel important. I struggle to feel or think about anything else. As I battle them and put them through their paces, rather than tiring and fizzling out, they strengthen and solidify. The idea becomes more defined and structured, and it burrows down from my brain, through my neck, and into my heart. If you're imagining the roots from the Upside Down of *Stranger Things*, you're spot on. If you have no idea what the Upside Down is, I need you to reconsider your life priorities.

As insane as it sounds, when these feelings or ideas or whatever you want to call them start to overcome me, the only way I have found to control them is to share them. The only way to save myself from being completely consumed by them is to get them outside of me and show them to others. Anyone who follows me on Facebook knows this to be true.

It's kind of like the creepy video tape from *The Ring*, only no one dies. I mean, not that I know of. Actually, I feel pretty confident none of my ideas have ever killed anyone. Knock on wood.

Honestly, I blame my Mormon mission for this. Just like any good little Mormon missionary, I said just about whatever I thought the Spirit was encouraging me to say, regardless of how insane it sounded. For better or worse, if I felt it, I said it. However, I did my best to avoid offering promises or prophesies of biblical proportions that I heard my black-name-tagged peers utter. Something about promising people their deepest desires if they kept XYZ commitment felt a little above my pay grade, but maybe I just lacked faith.

When I started to write this book, I felt bolstered by the confidence that this would be essentially like one big glorified Facebook post. I would simply just dump my thoughts, opinions, and ideas into one big Word document for someone to proofread and print out with a pretty cover on it. However, the deeper I got into the process, the more I realized that this is different. A Facebook post has a lifespan of one to three days before it is buried deep down in your feed. The only one to see it after that point would be your next blind date doing her or his due diligence Facebook research (read: stalking). I once wrote a post on Facebook that went Mormon viral, and it only lasted about six days. Tops. (More on that post later.)

As this manuscript got longer, it started to feel scarier. For me, the scariest part about writing a book like this is how permanent it feels. If I write a Facebook post when I'm in the thralls of passion that I later feel a little less passionate about, I don't need to worry about it. Even if my point of view completely changes from a post, I can simply shrug my shoulders and forget about it. A post is so temporary and in the moment. A post is deletable!

A book, on the other hand, feels like I'm getting these ideas tattooed on my face. Once these ideas and stories are printed, they can live on someone's shelf for however long they would like. *That freaks me out!*

Why? Because I'm a big believer in the importance of constantly learning new things and developing new ideas and opinions. In my mind, if your ideas and opinions aren't changing through the years as you meet new people, gain new knowledge, and have new experiences, you are doing something wrong. It scares me that my ideas in my late twenties could somehow be construed as representative of my thoughts, positions, and opinions for the rest of my life.

Though these fears and concerns are valid and justified, I choose to follow in the path of women whose words and stories have touched my life. Women like Ashley Mae Hoiland and Rachel Hunt Steenblik whose words, though far more poetic than mine and thick with hard-earned wisdom, felt like a warm arm around my shoulders. They reminded me of the women in my life who walk with me when they can and continue to love me when I must walk alone.

My life has not followed a traditional path. Honestly, I don't think anyone's has. Though some of my experiences draw more attention than others, I don't for one second think my experiences are more important than yours. At the end of the day, I think we will all end up in heaven having learned the same foundational principles in a thousand different ways.

In his talk "Be Ye Therefore Perfect—Eventually," Elder Holland shared a story of a priest written by Leo Tolstoy. This priest, a human trying his best but falling short, was under condemnation from the people around him because he was imperfect. If he was imperfect, so must be the principles he taught, they reasoned. To this, the priest cried:

> Attack me, [if you wish,] I do this myself, but [don't] attack . . . the path I follow. . . . If I know the way home [but] am walking along it drunkenly, is it any less the right way simply because I am staggering from side to side?
>
> . . . Do not gleefully shout, "Look at him! . . . There he is crawling into a bog!" No, do not gloat, but give . . . your help [to anyone trying to walk the road back to God.][2]

I think it is neat that we can still learn from the experiences of others even when they differ greatly from our own and when the people themselves are imperfect. Most of us will never win a beauty pageant that lands us a marriage to a king and in a prime position to save our entire nation from a prideful troll of a man. However, we still can learn volumes from Esther's story, and a girl can dream.

As you get deeper into this book and read my experiences, you will see that your life and my life are totally different. I hope you will keep reading. Actually, I hope you will keep *feeling*. More important than the words that I say are the feelings you feel when you read them. Maybe you will learn something that relates to what you are reading, and maybe you will learn something that differs completely. Regardless, I hope you will learn something.

Throughout these pages, I will share the stories, ideas, thoughts, and experiences that have made me who I am today. Who I am today is a pretty normal person. But I am happy. My hope is that this book will help you find a little more happiness in your life. When you finish the last page, I don't expect you to be brimming with joy. In fact, spoiler alert, you probably won't be. Why? Because that's not how true happiness works. Happiness is developed. Happiness is a strange but good cocktail of time, disappointments, do-overs, and hard work. When you finish the last page, my goal is for you to walk away having a plan in your mind as to how you will begin to develop more peace, happiness, and love in your life. And with a little luck, you'll feel a greater desire and drive that will motivate you to actually do something differently in your life. You could have the keys to the most elegant, well-designed, and perfectly made vehicle—(cough) '72 Bronco (cough)—but it will do you zero good until you fill it up with gas.

Some of these lessons I share are deeply personal to me. Personal both in nature and application. Luckily, I'm a millennial and, thanks to social media, fairly comfortable sharing personal experiences in a way that makes anyone over forty-five cringe. I recognize that some of the things I share may only apply to me, but chances are there is at least one other person who can learn from them. If something you read doesn't sit right with you, I hope you will at least give it a place to rest in your heart for just a moment before kicking it out. Maybe, with a little conversation, you will decide you can jive with this new idea more than you expected. But if it ends up being like the vast majority of blind dates I have been on, no worries. All you need to do is say, "Thanks, but no thanks," and just move on. Just like in dating, no matter how weird you think a person/idea is, there is usually someone out there who will love that person/idea. Just because an idea doesn't sit right with you doesn't mean it can't be exactly what someone else is looking for.

Notes

1. Elizabeth Gilbert, "Your Creative Genius," TED Talk, February 2009, https://www.ted.com/talks/elizabeth_gilbert_on_genius.
2. Jeffrey R. Holland, "Be Ye Therefore Perfect—Eventually," *Ensign*, November 2017.

Chapter 1

Middle School and High School Are Brutal

The day before my sixth birthday, the summer of 1995, Disney released its cartoon version of Pocahontas in theaters. Pocahontas is my eleventh great-grandma, so this movie felt like straight up family history to my little heart. As we walked out of the theater, I was bursting with pride and even asked my mom if anyone at Disney had contacted our family to make sure they got the facts straight. I would be lying if I didn't admit I felt a little bummed they didn't want our names, her descendants, in the credits. I was very proud to be the granddaughter of a Disney princess, especially the one who could talk to animals, high dive, and negotiate peace talks. But I understood that not even Disney was perfect, so I forgave them for the oversight and milked my newfound famous-by-association status for all it was worth.

So that fall, I started first grade. When I wasn't chasing my crush, Cory, I was catching worms in the schoolyard with my girls. It had just rained so it was easy to find the slimy creatures. We pressed some dirt in the base of a Dixie cup that we smuggled out of our classroom and laid a pair of worms on top. I remember stroking the back of one of the worms and announcing to my friends, "This one is a girl, and the other is a boy." One of the girls in the group was skeptical that I could read the sex of the worms—and rightly so. I, fully aware that I had no idea what I was talking about, looked at her and said, "Pocahontas is my eleventh great-grandma." A friend next to me quickly added, "She can talk to animals." With that, the doubter became a believer, and we went on making plans for the worm babies that we were sure would be arriving any day now.

Those early years of school were easy. I had plenty of friends, and the clear majority of them totally believed whatever insane story (read: lie) I told them. I don't remember much, but I remember usually having someone to play with and winning so many "first to call in" contests on Radio Disney that I got banned from playing anymore because I "needed to give the other kids a try." (If my publisher would let me, I would put an eye-roll emoji face here. It's not my fault other six- to eight-year-olds couldn't dial as quickly as I could.) Luckily, I was still allowed to call in and request the "Macarena." My older sisters and I spent our summer days blading to our friends' homes in the neighborhood and getting into the kind of trouble every kid should get into.

When I was seven, there was a family in our ward whose cat had kittens, and I wanted one desperately. Knowing that my parents would for sure turn down my request for a second pet (I already had a dog), I devised a plan and recruited my older sisters to my cause. While my parents were both at work, I sent my sisters to the store to buy kitty litter, food, and toys. While they spent every penny they had saved to their names, I walked the few blocks to the cat owner's house. I knocked on the door and told them that my dad wanted to surprise my mom with a kitten for her upcoming birthday and he asked me to pick one up while he was at work. For the next two days, my sisters and I blissfully kept our secret kitty in a small cubby in the wall next to my bed. It all went beautifully until the cat couldn't keep its darn mouth shut one night while my dad was tucking me into bed. When he asked if I heard the noise coming from the wall, I said I for sure didn't. Unsure if it was a rat, a skunk, or some other wild animal, he carefully opened the cubby door and, much to his surprise, pulled out a small kitten from a perfectly manicured litter box and pile of kitten toys. Before I knew it, I was standing on the cat owner's porch in my Little Mermaid nightgown, explaining why I had to give the cat back. I remember it being dark and pouring rain, but my dad says I'm just being dramatic.

Now that I'm about the same age as my dad was when this all went down, I wonder what was going through his head that night. Surely, he was annoyed and likely embarrassed . . . I mean, I did con a ward member. However, I like to think that as he and my mom were lying in bed, they had a good laugh about it and felt a little proud of the wild, brave, and sometimes sneaky and scheming little women they were raising.

And that, my friends, it a pretty good picture of the simple and happy life I lived up until third grade.

In third grade, my world got flipped upside down and turned inside out. Early in the school year, my parents decided my mom was going to move to New York and go back to school. She had been running her own interior design company for years, but she was going to get her degree at the Fashion Institute of Technology in New York City. I was only eight at the time, so I didn't understand all of the details or how long this decision had been in the works, but I remember it feeling fast. My dad learned how to use a curling iron, daycare was arranged for my nine-month-old baby sister, and then my mom was gone.

If you're thinking my mom left us or that my parents were separating, you wouldn't be alone. Much of the neighborhood and even my teachers thought the same thing. When my teacher found out that my mom had moved, I started receiving special privileges. For example, if I said I had a tummy ache, my teacher would let me sit in her private office and eat a peanut butter sandwich no matter what time of day it was or what we were doing. It was incredible. When one of my classmates asked to do the same, my teacher responded, "No. Only Rosie gets to because her mommy isn't here anymore." I was pretty stoked about this new advantage, but the truth is my mom didn't leave us and my parents weren't getting a divorce. They had plans for us to take turns flying between Salt Lake and New York every few weeks. But the fact that my sisters and I laid out our mom's things that she didn't take with her on our living room floor and essentially cast lots for who got what tells me we didn't totally grasp what was going on. Though my dad made us put everything back, I was hopeful that I would one day be reunited with my selected inheritance of scrapbook paper and teardrop faux-pearl clip-on earrings.

My parents were acting on revelation as quickly as they received it. They were running into the darkness with faith that He would light the way. Not long after our mom moved to New York, my parents felt like it could be a good experience for the whole family. Excited for our new adventure, my sisters and I soon flew back East to join our mom. We left our comfy cozy home and neighborhood in Sandy, Utah, for a remodeled fire station converted into an apartment in Irvington, New York. Living in the fire station home were my mom, my four sisters, my aunt, my four cousins, and me. With both moms studying in the city, my sisters, cousins, and I had a lot of time to ourselves.

When I think about that little eight-year-old me, I wish I could just squeeze her. So much in her life changed so drastically so fast. I know she struggled to process all the change because she went to the nurse's office every day complaining about a nonexistent stomach ache. I would lay on the paper-covered cot with my back to the door and clutch my stomach. I needed to make sure the nurse believed I was sick, and the fetal-position-stomach-clutch was my go-to move. I remember closing my eyes and essentially playing dead as kids from my class would walk by in the hall in between classes. When the bell rang, signaling that I made it through one more school day, the nurse would say, "See you tomorrow, Rosie," and I would pop up and be on my way. Once at home, my sisters and I did our best to keep busy. Since we no longer could ride our bikes around our neighborhood, we spent a lot time walking to and from the convenience store called This 'N That a few blocks away, walking the park down the street from us that ran along the bank Hudson River, and I started casually shoplifting Beanie Babies from the toy store on the corner.

When our dad finally came to New York a few weeks later, we moved again, this time to an extended-stay Marriott in White Plains, New York. My dad was having trouble finding work, and my parents were having even more trouble finding someone to rent to a family with five kids and no solid job. We fasted a lot as a family during our three-month hotel stay. After school, while our parents were still in the city, my sisters and I would walk to the nearby Galleria Mall. We had only the few dollars we had earned and saved, but we liked being there all the same. When we lived in Sandy, Utah, we would often take the bus to Cottonwood Mall. Maybe something about the Galleria Mall with its florescent lights and shiny floors felt familiar to us, but maybe we just had nowhere else to go. When we had to go back to the hotel, we would wander the halls, take turns playing simple games on the one hotel computer just outside the laundry room, and watch our sister Hailey draw carbon copies of our favorite Disney characters. For Christmas that year, I bought Hailey a tiny *101 Dalmatians* flip book because there were a zillion pictures in there for her to re-create.

After months of disappointment, tremendous pressure, and determined faith, my dad was able to secure a job at the same advertising firm as our bishop. We moved to a rental home a couple of blocks from the Scarsdale Metro North train station. When I think of that little yellow home with green carpet, I think of the cozy hiss of radiators in the winter, starring in our basement reenactment of *Joseph and the Amazing Technicolor Dreamcoat* as Potiphar's wife (not sure why I was always the scandalous character in our little plays, but I'm kinda proud of it), and playing Suicide Barbies on the back balcony. Suicide Barbies is a super-not-PC game where you tie floss around your Barbies and then try to throw them from your balcony onto the roof of the garage behind your house. Then you reel them in, try to spot where their limbs landed in the yard, and throw them out again. Warning: only play Suicide Barbies with the permission of the owner of the Barbies. Learned that lesson the hard way. Also, maybe consider calling it something like "X-Treme Sports Barbies" instead.

The Card girls soon became regulars at the pizzeria at the bottom of the street. We'd save up our babysitting money and blow it on pepperoni slices and cans of soda. One day, my sisters and I were walking home from the pizzeria when we noticed a Metro North conductor's hat on the train tracks. We decided that it only made sense for me to scale the tall fence that was meant to keep little idiots like us off the train tracks and retrieve our discovery. I carefully stepped over the rails, vaguely recalling something about death by electrocution if you touch the third rail, and grabbed the hat. Much to my surprise and exactly like it happens in all of the movies, there was suddenly a train coming around the bend. Treasure in hand, I scurried back up and over the fence, ripping my pants in the process.

I have lots of cozy memories of this time. The Japanese kids we shared a bus stop with often brought hard candies for us to suck on, which I much preferred over the individually wrapped seaweed portions they often munched. My teacher was a kind woman who smelled like she had been marinating in coffee for the last thirty years. Her desk and, more importantly, her coffee pot were in the back corner of the room. When she would leave her desk and move throughout the room, the thick and warm smell would follow her. I loved every whiff of it. I became close friends with a sweet Catholic girl who lived across the street. We played Spice Girls in her backyard a lot, but it usually ended in a fight because I wanted to be the Spice Girls' pet dog, and she didn't super enjoy playing with a friend who only crawled around on all fours panting and barking. Weird.

A new home meant a new school. Three different schools in third grade ain't for the weak. Kids are resilient, and with time, my sisters and I got tougher. We learned how to hunker down and make new friends quickly. However, life was different now. In Sandy, I had endless friends who were just like me. I never questioned whether I fit in—I just belonged. In New York, I eventually made friends, but I was the new kid and I was very different. I wasn't enrolled in an afterschool catechism program or Hebrew school. I couldn't say "bat mitzvah," let alone understand what it was, nor was I able to have playdates after Sunday Mass.

I know most people move at least once in their early years, and I know anyone who grew up in a military family is probably rolling their eyes right out of their head by this point. But here is the deal, even if you have lived in the same home your entire life and have had the same friends since infancy, I know you can relate to this feeling of longing for love and acceptance you once felt, but now have lost. I know everyone feels this change, whether they recognize it or not, because I know everyone, one way or another, is searching for love and acceptance. As humans, it is just what we do. As far as I am concerned, the girl posting a sexy selfie on Instagram and the woman busting her butt to get that raise at work are doing the same thing: searching for love, acceptance, and, in turn, happiness.

In middle school and high school, the search looks like a popularity contest. It's who makes what team, who got asked to what dance, who sits where at lunch, and who gets invited to what party. In college and young adult years, it's clubs, teams, groups, or sororities. Later, it's play groups, book clubs, and luncheons. Does it mean we're shallow monsters running essentially the same rat race over and over? No. It means we are humans having a continually human experience. Everyone, whether you are willing to acknowledge it or not, wants and needs love. We all look for it and find it in different places. So where in the world does this constant hunger come from?

Before we came to this earth, we were spirits. We were spirits who lived with Heavenly Parents, a Mother and Father who loved us perfectly. They loved us for who we were and who we had the potential to become. Our love cups were overflowing. Because They love us to the moon and back and want the very best for us, these sweetie perfect parents sent us down to earth. On earth we get rad bodies, just like Them, and we get to have experiences that help us learn and grow. But there is one problem. Earth is not heaven. We are here and They are there.

Though our wee human brains can't remember life before this one, I think our spirits can. Our spirits remember what that ultimate love and acceptance felt like and they miss it. Elaine Cannon called it an "eternal homesickness."[1] Can we honestly blame them? We know true love and acceptance exists. We just forgot where to find it.

Think of it like this. Imagine we all have matching flip flops that we wore around all summer. At the end of the summer, we gather for a party at the beach. We kick off our matching flip flops in a line at the edge of the beach because everyone knows walking in sand with flip flops is basically a death wish. At the end of the party, we all gather at the mass of identical flip flops and begin the process of figuring out whose is whose. It might take some time, and it will for sure take trying on a few pairs, but eventually we would all be able to figure it out. Sure, if the size is right, you can get away with wearing someone else's flip flops, but there is something that just doesn't feel right. When you slip into your flip flops, there is something familiar about the fit. It just feels right.

That's kinda what I think we are doing. We know what true belonging feels like. Sure, there some things we can do that make us feel pretty good. Getting asked to prom by one of the popular guys is exciting, or so I'm told (shrug emoji). Growing your Instagram following can feel pretty good too. But at the end of the day, those things are kind of like walking around in someone else's flips. It's fine, but something in us knows this isn't the real thing. Do you know what I mean? It's like taking a swig of Mr. Pibb when you ordered a Dr. Pepper. Something just ain't right.

For me, in middle school and high school, I was sure I would be happy if the cool girls wanted me around more and if the cool guys wanted me around at all.

FOMO is real. When I was in high school, I would spend Friday after school calling around to see where the girls were hanging out. "Sorry, Rosie. She's at so-and-so's house." Calls so-and-so's house. "Oh, sorry, Rosie. They're at so-and-so's house." Sometimes I would find them and meet up, but sometimes not. If not, I would feel sad, but I could play with my dog or play an absurd amount of Sims, and my weekend would go on. I didn't really have to deal with FOMO until Monday at lunch, when all my friends talked about what they did over the weekend. I cringe to think how difficult it must be for middle and high schoolers of today because, thanks to social media, they get real-time updates and or even a live feed of what everyone is doing every moment without them. That has got to *suck*!

In her book *Braving the Wilderness* (a book I personally think should be on the "How to Be a Good Human" required reading list), Brené Brown talks about the difference between "fitting in" and "belonging." To differentiate between the two, Brené spoke to the experts on the topic: middle schoolers. This is what they taught her:

- *"Belonging* is being somewhere where you want to be, and they want you. *Fitting in* is being somewhere where you want to be, but they don't care one way or another.
- *Belonging* is being accepted for you. *Fitting in* is being accepted for being like everyone else.
- If I get to be me, I belong. If I have to be like you, I fit in."[2]

Mic drop.

If you've survived middle or high school, you get this. If you've joined a club, married into a family, been on a team, started a new job, or really just ever interacted with any group of humans, you get this.

The difference between belonging and fitting in hits home with me because in high school I, on some level, fit in. My friends were cheerleaders and on the dance team. We sat together at lunch and hung out most weekends. By most appearances, I fit in, but I can promise you I very seldom felt like I belonged.

In a lot of ways, I felt like I was being tolerated. I rarely felt truly wanted and loved. If I called enough homes, maybe I could intercept my group of friends and hang out with them. Rarely did I receive a phone call inviting me to meet them somewhere to hang. Maybe it is the curse of being young and in high school, or maybe it was the combination of my personality and the kids around me, but there was something about my place in my friend group that didn't feel secure or safe.

When my family moved back to Salt Lake suddenly during the last six weeks of sixth grade, I was heartbroken. After four years, I had found a happy social home at school. I was in the band, and being in the band was cool in NY. My best friends, a Jewish girl named Jessica and a Catholic boy named Paul, both lived on my block. We would meet up after school and walk to the pizzeria next to Paul's dad's jewelry store and share slices. The brother and sister who operated the deli up the street knew us by name and would always ask, "Bacon, egg, and cheese on a roll, or toasted plain bagel with butter?" when I walked in.

When my parents announced we were moving back to Utah, I wanted to be a good sport. I had high hopes that this transition would be easier. I was familiar with the "new girl" experience and thought moving back to Utah would be much easier considering this time mostly everyone would be just like me. So I said my tearful goodbyes to my friends and got ready to move again. The morning of the move, I found a litter of kittens in the wooded area behind our home. I considered smuggling one in our Suburban for the cross-country drive but decided the babies were too young to leave their mother.

The first day in my new Utah school, I couldn't help but recognize how many blonde kids there were. I quickly made friends with a freckled little girl named Hailey and a pure towhead named Elise. Elise, Hailey, and I were in the same ward, and they were kind enough to introduce me to all of their friends. Hailey was sweet and kind and had the kind of laugh that makes you feel good when you hear it. Elise had a wit and a sass that was well beyond her years. She reminded me of my friends back in New York, and I felt like we made a good team.

Elise's favorite animal was the llama, and the toy store up the street had a *giant* stuffed animal llama. We decided to have a lemonade stand to raise the necessary funds. Not long after our grand opening, I realized we were never going to raise enough money for the llama using a standard lemonade stand business model. We needed something to really draw the people in. I flipped our signs over and in big black sharpie letters wrote *RAISING MONEY FOR CANCER RESEARCH*. Game changer. Before the afternoon was through, we had eighty-some-odd dollars that we promptly spent on the giant toy llama. As we walked home taking turns carrying the massive animal on our backs, I felt pretty smug, like we had performed a pretty cool trick. Clearly, we lied through our teeth to lots of people that afternoon, but I will always remember lying to my Primary teacher. I knew what I was doing wasn't right, but I don't think I understood how creepy and messed up our actions really were.

Before anyone gets all riled up, I'll have you know I have donated to cancer-related causes for several years. My company has donated nearly $10,000 to families of children fighting cancer in Primary Children's hospital. I've paid back the $80, with interest.

Somewhere around the time of scamming my neighbors for an oversized stuffed animal, I started growing—and I started growing fast. I went from being an average-sized kid to one of the tallest in the class seemingly overnight, but I didn't gain a pound. I was always a lanky skinny kid. We have family video of my dancing to "Boot Scootin' Boogie" on skinny legs that look like they're one reckless twirl away from snapping. My new height only further exaggerated my thinness.

My frame was so extreme that everyone from my doctors to choir teacher started asking questions about how much I was eating. Was I overexercising? Was I skipping meals? And they weren't the only ones who noticed. The bully boys noticed too. I didn't totally understand what these leading questions were alluding to until I looked up *anorexic* and *bulimic* in the Clayton Middle School library dictionary when the bully boys started shouting it at me in the halls.

By the time I hit middle school and high school, I was familiar with the subtle art of girl bullying. Subtle yet sharp comments, exclusion, and gossip are some of our favorite tactics, but the loud and physical bullying techniques of bully boys were new to me.

In New York, when a teen or child talks back to a superior, when a kid gets in an adult's face with attitude, they refer to it as being "fresh." My predominantly Italian Catholic girl crew were basically experts on getting fresh. When the boys started bullying in Utah, my brave little heart, though scared, couldn't help but stand up for itself. I got real fresh. I didn't know why, but there was something in me that just couldn't sit quietly by and let what I saw as injustice play out before me. I had to say something even if saying something put me into harm's way. People told me to just ignore them and to not talk back. In their minds, by standing up for myself, I was only encouraging the bullying, and that somehow made it all my fault.*

> *Let me shout loud enough for the people in the back, if you are being teased, bullied, or hurt, IT IS NOT YOUR FAULT. No one *asks* to be hurt, just like no one is *forced* to hurt someone. Bullies, of any type or seriousness, are in charge of their choices and will be held accountable for their own freaking actions. Teaching a victim to change to avoid abuse is like getting mad at someone who got food poisoning for eating at the offending restaurant. When it comes to abuse, in any shape or form, we need to be sure we go to the root of the problem. Sure, victims can do things to protect themselves, but doesn't it just make sense to fix the actual problem? Let's focus on putting out the house fire rather than being mad at the house for being flammable.
>
> In a BYU devotional called "Agency, Accountability, and the Atonement of Jesus Christ: Application to Sexual Assault," Benjamin M. Ogles paints a perfect parallel from a personal experience. He tells about a time that his car was broken into in the middle of the night. He immediately started asking himself what he could have done differently to prevent the crime. Should he have parked in a different place? Did he remember to lock the doors? Essentially, he started to blame himself for someone else's crime.
>
> > No matter where I had parked, how naïve I had been, or whether I had locked the doors or not, no one has the right to take things from my car without my permission. I was not responsible for the theft. Yet I automatically took the blame because I could imagine things that I

thought I should have done differently. . . .

. . . The perpetrator is responsible for their actions. A victim was deprived of their agency, and they are not accountable for what happened to them without their consent—no matter what they were wearing, where they were, or what happened beforehand. They did not invite, allow, sanction, or encourage the assault.[3]

As a teen-year-old who thought all adults were always right, I believed this. I believe that this was all somehow my fault. I believed that if I weren't so tall and skinny, I would be happier. If my body looked more like a woman and less like a deacon, the bullies wouldn't bully, I would be loved, and I would be happy. In my mind, my body was bad, and the way God made me was not the way I should be. Unfortunately, I'm not alone in this experience. It especially breaks my heart when I hear of our LGBTQ+ brothers and sisters erroneously thinking that they were born broken. God doesn't make mistakes. I believe our Heavenly Mother and Father were mindful to every detail when creating us. We are their favorite creation! Which is pretty incredible when you think that these are the same masterminds behind golden retriever puppies, the Maldives, tree blossoms, and peaches.

Verbally fighting back was how I tried to protect myself, but I also tried to fix the problem—the problem, wrongly of course, being me. I ate and I ate. Conveniently, because I was growing so much and a standard teen, I was starving and could pound through an above-average amount of food. I started carrying food with me so I could eat in front of teachers and hopefully stall their inappropriately personal questions regarding my eating habits. Whenever I ate with a group of people, I made sure to serve myself bigger helpings than anyone else and always take seconds, regardless of how hungry I was.

I'm willing to bet at least one of you is feeling pretty annoyed at this point and thinking, *If you're staying skinny and hungry, why are you complaining? #skinnygirlproblems*, or *Count your many blessings. I wish I could eat like a bottomless pit and be skinny.* I know. I get it. We live in a culture that values thinness over thickness. We're force-fed the thin ideal every time we watch a movie, turn on the TV, open a magazine, scroll social media, or sit down to family dinner with a judgy aunt.

The thin ideal is an awful marketing tactic used by companies to sell more product.

Wanna know what else is a marketing tactic? "Real women have curves" or any other movement that simply turns the heat from one group of women to another and creates divisions amongst us.

These marketing campaigns do not empower us—they distract and confuse us. They distract us by continually encouraging us to believe that the ultimate goal we can accomplish is to be beautiful. The Dove Real Beauty campaign is the perfect example. Dove spends millions of dollars to make viral videos celebrating all women as beautiful. Is it feel-good? Freak, yes! Does it fall completely short? Absolutely.

One of their most popular videos is shot hidden-camera style. The cameras focus on the entrance to a large building in some random city. The building has two entrances right next to each other. Over one door hangs a sign that says "beautiful" over the other hangs a sign that reads "average." This is apparently duplicated in cities all over the world. The video shows various women approaching the doors, their confused reactions, and then hesitant choices of which door they enter. In the video, edited nicely to fit Dove's messaging, initially most women choose to walk through the door labeled "average." As the piece progresses, they show diverse women encouraging one another to go through the "beautiful" door. A mother yanks her daughter from the path leading to the "average" door and encouragingly waves to others as they blaze their way through the "beautiful" door. You wanna know the first thing I thought after watching this? If the answer is no, too bad I'm going to tell you. I thought, *Where the heck is the "smart" door? Or the "capable" door? The "hardworking" door? The "clever" door? Congrats on your "beautiful" door, Dove. I'm more interested in the "tough and good at stuff" and "doing my best to be a good person" door.*

In her TEDxSaltLakeCity talk entitled "Body Positivity or Body Obsession? Learning to See More & Be More," Dr. Lindsay Kite of Beauty Redefined said, "Girls and women aren't only suffering from the unattainable ways beauty is being defined, they're suffering because they are being *defined* by beauty. They are *bodies* first and *people* second."[4]

Besides the feel-good factor of the video, there is one redeeming element. If applied to principles that matter more, the words of the women they interview are pretty powerful. One woman says, "Am I choosing because of what's constantly bombarded at me? What I'm being told that I should accept? Or am I choosing because that's what I really believe?" I get that we are constantly told our most important contribution to the world is our appearance, but, deep down, is that what you really believe? I hope the answer is HECK NO! But if not, keep reading. You can keep reading really regardless of what your answer is.

Satan understands that women are Bad-A powerhouses who get crap done while leading others to do the same. And because he is an insecure fragile shell of a being, we scare the crap out of him. If Satan can get us to focus on our appearance, whether in a self-loathing or in a prideful way, he can distract us from becoming and developing into the Bad-A forces for good whom Jesus died for to enable us to become. Let it be known that Satan isn't letting anyone off the hook here. This guy is a grade-A jerk, and he doesn't play favorites. All women, regardless of size or appearance, are fighting this battle. The girls I lived with while modeling battled body issues just as intense as the curvier girls I went to high school with. Categorizing women and pinning us against one another for competition and comparison only makes the fight harder. Other women are *not* the enemy. Satan is.

So why is it bad that my little high school life was consumed with proving to people that I ate? Because I wasn't always hungry, and I, like any other woman, am more than my body and I'm definitely more than what I eat. I am now in my late twenties. It has been *years* since someone accused me of having an eating disorder, both because my bones don't exactly stick out like they used to and because that's not a normal thing adults say to one another. However, I still fight to overcome these bad habits. I still catch myself taking seconds when I don't really want them. While writing this book, I went with my boyfriend on a trip to New Mexico to visit his cousin. On the last day, I woke up early to watch my boyfriend compete in a bike race. I ate a protein bar on the ride over. After the race, we went back to their house to pack up. They offered us sandwiches, but I wasn't feeling great, so I politely declined. The day went on and we left a couple of hours later. *Multiple* times that afternoon, as we drove from his cousin's home, I nervously commented on how his cousins probably think I have an eating disorder simply because they didn't see me eat that morning. I promise I don't think I'm so skinny that people make this assumption. This is just to prove bad habits planted and cultivated in our early years can plague us long after our frontal lobes fully develop.

Through all of these confusing messages and deeply intense and personal battles, I find hope in the fact that we are resilient. I find great courage in the story of Eve. Eve made a choice that was extremely difficult and probably deeply confusing. Yet she made her choice and stepped into the world. For little high school Rosie, doing her best to survive and navigate her world, courage looked like standing up for herself. Talking back to the bullies. Getting *real* fresh with them. In *Pride and Prejudice*, Jane Austen's words perfectly described what I've felt for a long time, "There is a stubbornness about me that never can bear to be frightened at the will of others. My courage always rises at every attempt to intimidate me."[5]

Sometimes my efforts to fight back and protect myself enabled me to be the last one standing. One day, my bully sauntered into our choir class, noticed me, greeted me with "bulimic anorexic b****," and then proceeded to sit in the chair directly in front of me. As he turned his back to me to sit down, I leaned forward and pulled his chair out from underneath him. His big footballer body came loudly crashing to the ground. The startled and annoyed choir teacher looked up and told him to stop messing around and to get in his seat. Was this the healthiest or smartest way to deal? No. Does twenty-eight-year-old Rosie wish she could fist bump thirteen-year-old Rosie in that moment? Yes.

Sometimes my efforts didn't leave me winning and on my feet. I can't remember what verbal exchange took place that led to this event, but I know I responded to one of the footballers in a way he didn't like. In the middle of the cafeteria, surrounded by our peers, he pinned me to the dirty floor, face down. He grabbed my right wrist and wrenched it behind my back. I thrashed all ninety-five pounds of me around to get free. He then pressed his knee in the small of my back and tightened his grip around my wrist as he cranked it further up between my shoulder blades. Pain seared through my shoulder and arm. Feeling like I was moments away from my arm snapping and/or shoulder erupting, I yanked my head around desperately looking for help. I locked eyes with one of the "nice guys." This guy was my friend, but he was also friends with the easily threatened unstable human who was likely in a roid rage on my back. I'm sure the nice guy could see the pain I was in as I, with tears in my eyes, screamed, "*HELP ME!*" He looked away.

The feeling of crumbs on the floor pressing into my cheek. The burning pull of my skin as his hand tightened around my wrist. The pressure of his knee on my spine. The audible reaction of the kids nearby. All of these make up the tornado of emotions, feelings, and memories of that moment. With all of that spinning around me, when the "nice guy" looked away, everything in my brain went still. In that moment, I decided that for the rest of my life, no matter how big and scary the bullies of the future would be, I would be braver than that "nice guy," and I would stand up for the little guy. Because I am one.

As strange as it may be to say that in that moment, face down on the East High cafeteria floor, I felt brave and hopeful, I did. Unfortunately, I didn't always feel that way. In fact, for the vast majority of my freshman and sophomore years, I felt small, scared, and miserable. Many nights I sobbed myself to sleep. Silently, of course, because any noise would have ended with a swat in the face from a sister in the bunk bed next to me or a foot in the back from the sister in the bunk bed below me—a practice I, too, regularly engaged in. (Five girls shared one bedroom, bathroom, and closet, but I'll save those war stories for another time.) I distinctly remember praying that I wouldn't wake up. "Please, Heavenly Father, just let me come home. Please let me die tonight in my sleep. Please let me come home. I'm done. Please." On the outside, I was the Beehive completing her Personal Progress while babysitting the vast majority of the Primary. On the inside, I was deeply depressed and casually contemplating suicide. In my young mind, high school was either never going to end or it would end me.

As I look back on these hard years, I know and remember really happy times. I had friends and peers who were kind and good to me. After not making the cheer squad or the dance team my sophomore year, I tried out and made the cheer team my junior year. I want to be clear that there were good times. However, there was something about the hard times and the dark feelings that smothered my ability to live in the good. I struggled to step out from underneath the dark clouds and really enjoy the sunlight.

I think it is also important to acknowledge that I was likely surrounded by others who were having similar experiences that I may have contributed to by action or ignorance. One of the most painful things about my own experience with anxiety and depression is how much it limits my ability to help others. When I'm pulled inward and in a place of fear, I'm consumed by my own issues and, in turn, less able to offer the help to others that I wish someone would offer me. So to anyone that I hurt, left out, ignored, or said something rude to in middle and high school: I'm so sorry.

There were so many people who loved and supported me through this time. First and foremost, my parents. A close second was a young mom in my ward, Allison Grant Dayton. I babysat for the Dayton family every chance I got. I loved Devin, Jake, and baby Lukey like they were my siblings. I also really loved their treat drawers and frozen pizza stash. Allison ran a jewelry business out of their home, and soon she hired me to help her. While stringing necklaces and soldering rings, Allison would ask me about my life and listen. Bless her soul for listening to my drama and heartbreak. She for sure offered incredible wisdom and council, but after all of these years, it is the memory of simply feeling loved and heard that has stuck with me.

It has been over fifteen years since I worked with Allison in her basement. To this day, Allison still plays an important role in my life. More than once I have texted her with a heavy heart late at night. Allison made it clear, through her actions early on, that she loved me and believed in me regardless of the ideas I had or the mistakes I made. She saved me when I was young, and she saves me still today.

I hope you can find your Allison. I hope I can be someone's Allison.

Hey, little sis, if you're reading this and you in any way relate to these feelings of desperation, I beg you to talk to someone. Please tell an adult you trust. A teacher, parent, Church leader, coach, or anyone who loves you. This is not a weight you were designed to carry alone. There is help. This doesn't have to last forever, but it's usually not something you can just pray away. As much as I believe in the doctrine of Taylor Swift, simply "shaking it off" doesn't apply here. If the person you tell reacts poorly, I need you to tell someone else. I know it's scary and hard and makes you feel vulnerable, but you are brave and strong. Getting help when you need it is one of the bravest and smartest things we can do.

If you're reading this and struggling to relate in the slightest, then please, let this be a lesson to you that not everyone is having the same experience. These types of situations are beautiful opportunities to really live our baptismal covenants. Mourn with those who mourn. When Mary wept at the feet of the Savior, mourning Lazarus's death, how did Christ react? Did He say, "Stop being dramatic. I would fix it if you would just calm down and listen to me"?

John 11:35: "Jesus wept."

Maybe high school makes you feel like you're on top of the world! You have great friends, you're on the team, you're getting the grade, and you're on your A game. But there is probably someone very close to you having a very hard time. My guess is that people who knew me in high school would be shocked to know I was on some level suicidal. In no shape or form am I saying you should feel guilty for the life you are living. In fact, I'm saying just the opposite. I'm saying you should be immensely grateful for the experience you have been given. When we are grateful for what we have, we acknowledge and show respect to those who have not. We are also in a position to give and serve those who have less than us. Because we never really know what the person next to us is dealing with, maybe try to be just a hair gentler with the people around you. Especially if you are in the trenches of high school where there is so much internal bleeding.

Woof. This is heavy. In writing this, I felt nervous that maybe the sassy fourteen-year-old in me is just trying to stick it to my bullies and have the ultimate last word. I texted three of my healthy and trusted friends—Lee, Mags, and Teen. "This bullying stuff is pretty heavy. Should I include it? How detailed should I be?" They all responded with "WRITE IT," and here's why.

1. I know that there will be women—little women in school or older women in life—dealing with bullying who will read this.

My hope is that by reading this, you can see that there is life after bullying. You can and you will get out of this phase with time and action.

2. I hope that anyone who reads this while quietly struggling with self-loathing thought patterns and/or depression will reach out to someone and get the help and love they deserve.

3. This is a crucial part of my story, because it was what drove me to find a way out.

For me, part of my solution was leaving traditional high school. I recognize that not everyone has that option. You may not be able to completely get away from your bullies, but you can put them in perspective.

If you need to feel brave, learn and study your underdog predecessors.

I am the fourth of five daughters of two artists who care little for sports. So while many of my peers grew up learning stories of the great athletes of our time, I learned about strong women. Women like my Grandma Romney, who on her very first day of school decided she didn't approve of the teacher's methods and informed her, "I won't be coming back." One of my favorite stories is of my who-knows-how-many-great-grandmothers, who was a convert in the early days of the Church. Shortly after she gave birth, a mob started tearing through her town. She sat in her front room rocking her newborn when the leader of the mob and his trolls came crashing through her front door.

"How old be your baby?" the coward in blackface said.

I'm sure it was no secret to her that mobs raped, beat, and murdered LDS women and men. Any normal human would have shuddered in fear, frozen, screamed, ran, or any combo of the above. But not this woman in this moment.

I imagine her standing, babe in arms, as she addressed the mob. She commands the kind of strength and power that is deeper than simply being physically intimidating.

"He was born the same day you started this harassment, *John Boynton*."

That's right. She straight up *called him by name*. You wanna know how she knew his name? Because John F. Boynton, a rogue member of the Quorum of the Twelve Apostles, had baptized her not long before.

Bad boy Boynton and his minions left her home with their tails between their legs, and the whole mob left the town that day.

Giiiirrrrllll. My great-something-grandma is a "tough and good at stuff" woman. This is the kind of person I think of when I need strength. Stories of the heroic women and men long gone who battled bullies of all varieties give me courage. It is also nice to look at the everyday normal people around you facing challenges. Notice that others are armoring up each day. Maybe give yourself a break from your own battle and offer a little support in someone else's.

Now, can we talk about this story a little bit? I've been told this story as long as I can remember. This woman and her story really have gotten me through hard times. I knew I wanted to share her story with you guys, but there is an honest part of me that wonders how historically accurate it is. Is this just part of my family's faith-prompting folklore? Where did this story come from? Do we have any primary sources to back this one up? Even if we did have a first-hand account, how do we know Great-Something-Grandma didn't embellish it in her journal that night?

The truth is, we don't. Great-Something-Grandma lived in the mid-1800s, so home girl didn't have Snapchat or Insta stories. We have to take history's word for it. But guess what? I don't really care. Whether this story is 100 percent accurate, embellished, or just a really nice story someone made up along the way to teach us little Mormons to be brave doesn't diminish my ability to learn from it.

Not too many years ago, I was reading my journal from my younger years. It was painful—like when you turn on the camera of your phone and it is forward facing and your own reflection scares you painful. I was so dramatic, and there was stuff in there that just straight up wasn't true. Reading through this made me wonder what could have motivated me to embellish in my own journal. Who did I think I was fooling? The more I thought about it, the more I realized that I was trying to impress my posterity. Growing up Mormon means you grow up hearing and reading ancestors', pioneers', and Church leaders' journals. When you're encouraged to keep a journal at a young age, you can't help but expect that someday some little member of your posterity will be reading yours! Right? Maybe I'm the only one who had aspirations of fame amongst their future grandbabies as a tween, but whatever.

All of this made me think about our scriptures. I've talked to lots of people who I really respect as great and faithful minds within the Church who have very different ideas about the stories within the Book of Mormon. Sometimes it is hard for me to imagine that Nephi was able to remember word-for-word conversations between his dad and brothers that happened years before he actually recorded them—and that it would all be accurately understood and communicated when a complete stranger came along hundreds of years later to summarize it into a book. Realistically speaking, there is a lot of room for human error. I can totally see why a lot of people struggle with the Book of Mormon.

However, just like how I'm able to benefit from the story of my Bad-A great-something-grandma regardless of historically accuracy, I can benefit from reading from the Book of Mormon. At the end of the day, does it really matter? For me? Nope. I don't need the stories to be verified historic events to be blessed by the principles they teach. I mean, never say never, but I'll probably never need to cut a man's head off with a sword. But I can still learn from Nephi's example that sometimes God asks you to do things differently than what you have been taught to do all your life.

And now can we talk about Mr. Shady Shade, John Boynton? Look, I'm sure John was a good dude at some point. His Wiki page says he was a great missionary for the Church and served missions in Pennsylvania, Maine, and Massachusetts. Anyone who has had one of those post-mission dreams where you get called on a second mission has to have mad respect for the early missionaries who served multiple times. John was called to be one of the OG apostles on February 14, 1835, at the organization of the initial Quorum of Twelve Apostles.

In 1837, the Kirtland Safety Society, the Church-sponsored bank, failed. Basically, the prophet asked members to invest their assets into this bank. Then they started to make their own currency. When President Andrew Jackson rejected privately printed money for public land, the bank failed. The Saints were anything but well off during the Kirtland period, and this just made things a whole lot worse. A lot of the members felt mislead, and they were justifiably angry. John said his issues with the Church started with "the failure of the bank," which he had understood "was instituted by the will & revelations of God, & he had been told that it would never fail."[6]

I'm in no way justifying his actions. No matter how mad or Punk'd he felt, mobbin' people like he did makes him a bad dude in my book. But there is a part of me that feels bad for him, because I honestly can't blame him. If I was putting all of my money in the basket that the prophet asked me to, and then that basket went up in flames, I'd be mad. Go ahead and judge me for it, but I would. I think any realistic person can understand how the people who lost everything due to the bank failure would feel misled and tricked.

If this all went down in our times, I would bet $1,000 (privately printed) that someone in John's ward would have said in a super judgy voice, "He can leave the Church, but he clearly can't leave it alone." You know I'm right! I know I'm right because I've said that about people plenty of times. Ten bucks (again, privately printed) says you've said that about your "apostate" former roommate or cousin too.

I'd love you to consider this: Can we blame them, and do we really want them to leave the Church alone?

In an ideal world, everyone intimately involved in the gospel of Jesus Christ has a love cup that is overflowing. Hopefully, everyone at some point feels the burning in their bosom (which I legit thought was a fancy word for "butt" until well into my teens) our spirits hunger for. And hopefully, everyone at some point feels and understands the important role The Church of Jesus Christ of Latter-day Saints, as an institution, plays in the administration of the gospel of Jesus Christ.

As we all know, it is growing more and more common for people to feel hurt by members or the Church itself. Many feel let down and discouraged by policies or teachings.

Yes, it is easy to say, "It's their own darn fault for getting offended. The members are imperfect people trying to live a perfect gospel. They should know better than to let themselves get offended." Easy response? Yes. Most Christlike? I'm not convinced.

In one of my most favorite recent reads, *The Dance of Anger*, Dr. Harriet Lerner teaches the feelings are not valid or invalid. They just are.

[Feelings are] neither legitimate nor illegitimate, meaningful nor pointless. [Feelings] simply [are]. To ask, "Is my [feeling] legitimate?" is similar to asking, "Do I have the right to be thirsty? After all, I just had a glass of water fifteen minutes ago. Surely my thirst is not legitimate. And besides, what's the point of getting thirsty when I can't get anything to drink now, anyway?"

[Feelings are] something we feel. [They exist] for a reason and always [deserve] our respect and attention. We all have a right to *everything* we feel.[7]

People who have served and sacrificed within the Church for any extended period of time don't take leaving the Church lightly. Elder Uchtdorf taught, "Sometimes we assume it is because they have been offended or lazy or sinful. Actually, it is not that simple. In fact, there is not just one reason that applies to the variety of situations. Some of our dear members struggle for years with the question whether they should separate themselves from the Church."[8]

These people leave because they have sustained serious wounds and they no longer feel that the Church is a place where they can heal. *This is heartbreaking*, and when I've tried to put myself in their shoes and imagine the pain they feel, I feel nothing but love and compassion for them.

Sometimes those people feel at peace when they leave, and sometimes they don't. Clearly, our boy John initially fell in the latter category. Yes, it sucks to hear former members of our own crew rail on the Church and gospel that is so near to our hearts. I can vouch that it is very difficult to not take it personally. The good news is the Church can take it. In fact, the Church is weirdly good at taking it. If you don't believe me, you need to google the advertisement our classy Church paid for in the playbill for *The Book of Mormon* musical. Whoever came up with that comeback deserves to dust the dirt of their shoulders.

So if it's not our job to protect the Church from every mean tweet or Facebook post, then what is it? Funny you should ask, says Matthew 22:36–39:

Master, which is the great commandment in the law?
    Jesus said unto him, Thou shalt love the Lord thy God with all thy heart, and with all thy soul, and with all thy mind.
    This is the first and great commandment.

And the second is like unto it, Thou shalt love thy neighbor as thyself.

We simply (sometimes not so simply) need to love these people rather than judge them. The next time your former YW leader turned Church hater posts something against the Church on Facebook, focus on trying to feel Christ's love for her. As much as you may wish she would just leave the Church alone, remember that heaven will never leave her. Be like Jesus and really try to feel and understand, even on the smallest scale, the pain she is feeling. When you turn to Christ with a broken heart, does He ever respond with, "It's your own fault. You shouldn't be so sensitive"? Not the Jesus I know. As you try to respond to this person like He would, you will, with time, begin to feel His love for her and be better able to play a role in helping her feel His love for her too.

If a lamb is wandering into danger, does the shepherd call out, "You've gone too far this time. I'm sorry, but there is no way in heck I'm risking going after you"? Heck no! When a lamb is in danger, the shepherd does all that he can to get as close as possible to his little one and carefully guide her to safety. Christ is a very very good shepherd. He does not give up on people.

Don't believe me? I give you two once-shady dudes: Saul and Alma the Younger. I can only imagine the freaky stuff they both would have been posting on their Facebook walls! Possibly freakier would have been the comments made in response to their posts by angry members. As much as the members in their respective days must have wished that they would just leave the Church alone, Heaven never left them. Heaven followed after them, just like a good shepherd, and when the time and the condition of their hearts were right, they came back. And they came back straight up lit.

Christ loves us even when we're not easy to love. Thank Heaven. If He does it, we should at least try. All of this being said, as a side note, if you need to unfollow that former YW leader, no judgment here, sis. Sometimes the most loving thing you can do for yourself and others is simply unfollowing someone.

And with that, we'll return to our regular programming.

Notes

1. Elaine Cannon, "A Wonderful Adventure: Elaine Cannon," *Ensign*, April 1983.

2. Brené Brown, *Braving the Wilderness: The Quest for True Belonging and the Courage to Stand Alone* (New York: Random House, 2017), 160.

3. Benjamin M. Ogles, "Agency, Accountability, and the Atonement of Jesus Christ: Application to Sexual Assault" (Brigham Young University devotional, January 30, 2018), 6, speeches.byu.edu.

4. Lindsay Kite, "Our TED Talk: Body Positivity or Body Obsession? How to See More & Be More," *Beauty Redefined*, November 7, 2017, https://beautyredefined.org/tedtalk-body-positivity-obsession.

5. Jane Austen, *Pride and Prejudice* (London: Penguin Books, 1996), 170.

6. John Boynton, in Kirtland Council Minute Book, 184–86.

7. Harriet Lerner, *The Dance of Anger: A Woman's Guide to Changing the Patterns of Intimate Relationships* (New York: William Morrow, 2014), 3–4.

8. Dieter F. Uchtdorf, "Come, Join with Us," *Ensign*, November 2013.

Chapter 2

A "Model" Mormon

Ever since I was a wee lass, my parents have encouraged my sisters and I to work for whatever we wanted. I remember being a tiny girl and desperately wanting a Pocahontas Barbie. My mom told me that I could have the Barbie if I folded a white load of laundry. I distinctly remember feeling like she had just asked me to do the impossible. I remember the white load piled on my mom's bed that was bigger than me. But I worked at it and eventually got my Barbie.

When I was ten, my family was living in New York. When you walk past a New York deli with bacon, egg, and cheese bagels that rock this world every morning on your way to school and pass an authentic pizzeria that sells the best pizza you've ever had by the slice on the way home, you *need* a job. My first job in New York was walking my neighbor's giant sheepdog. The dog's human parents both worked in the city, so I would let it out after school and take it on a quick walk around the block. After a few weeks of dog walking, I had saved up quite a few dollars. I pulled out the yellow pages and looked up all the local horse stables. I made a list of the closest locations and called around to see how much it would cost to go for an hour ride. Much to my surprise, there was a stable less than a mile from my school and I had enough money to pay for an hour trail ride. I presented my findings to my parents and requested permission and a ride to the stable.

After my trail ride, as I waited for my mom to pick me up, I noticed there were five to seven girls my age running around with horse tack and grooming gear in their arms. They all had cute riding pants and boots with their long hair pulled back into low ponytails. They wove in an out of the various stable buildings with horses in tow. Some were preparing horses for rides while others sprayed off the big sweaty animals with a hose. Assuming that these girls were employees of the stable, not realizing that they all owned and were caring for their own horses, I found an adult woman who looked like she was somewhat in charge and asked if I could have a job too. When my mom arrived to pick me up, I excitedly ran to her car window, stood on the Suburban runner boards, and exclaimed, "I got a job!" and that I needed her to come back and pick me up in a few hours because I was starting right away! I would muck stalls and prepare horses for customers' riding lessons a couple of days after school for about three hours in exchange for one hour of riding a week. I was getting robbed, but I thought I was the luckiest girl in the world.

What does this have to do with anything? Well, mainly I just want you to know what a rad horse-obsessed ten-year-old I was, but also because that was the first of many times that I had a problem, did my research on solutions, and found a way to do what I wanted.

Fast-forward a few years to depressed high school Rosie. I knew I needed to find a way out, but I wasn't sure how. The summer of 2005, I was getting ready to start my junior year in high school at East High in Salt Lake City. A friend picked me up to go to lunch. On our way, we drove past the school and were surprised to see massive movie trailers, equipment, and people walking around the campus. We decided to pull over and check it out. We wandered the halls for a bit until we found someone with a clipboard—clipboards are always so official looking. Being the nosy person I am, I asked what they were doing. "We're filming a Disney Channel movie. The plot is kind of hard to explain, but, essentially, it's about high school, and it's a musical." I thought that sounded a little weird, but I didn't care. I wanted to be involved. With a few more questions, I weaseled my way into being a dancing extra in *High School Musical*.

I only spent a few days on set dancing in a pep rally and "Stick to the Status Quo," but I loved every second of it. Before my first day on set, I went shopping for the perfect wardrobe. Ultimately, I splurged for hot-pink tank top and shiny pea-green track jacket from Wet Seal. I was sure this fresh look would get me placed near the front.

If you have ever been on a movie set, you know that there is a lot of sitting around. Quick segments are shot over and over again. The giant lighting equipment can take hours to set up or move. During all of this down time, the extras were all rounded up in the school gymnasium. Kids read books and played cards on the bleachers to pass time. I found myself hanging around the two adults in charge of the extras. They sat at a table with walkie talkies, and I liked hearing the ins and outs of set coordination over the little speakers. As I sat and listened, I made friends with one of the adults. I found out that he was a casting director and had helped pick Zac Efron—though Zac Efron was just a normal kid at that point, and he was shorter than me, so I wasn't super impressed. At some point during these hangout times, the cast director said that given how tall and skinny I was, I should consider modeling.

Now, I really liked this guy. He was nice to us kids and seemed really good at his job, but when he suggested I look into modeling, I thought, *He may not be very smart.* Why? Because I knew what models looked like! Models were mega babes with rocking bods. In my mind, my body was the very worst part of me. For sure, it wasn't something worth highlighting or celebrating. As much as I didn't think I was model material, I couldn't help but fantasize about escaping my current life and running away to a sparkling glamorous model life.

Initially, I looked into modeling on the local level. I found an agency that signed me up for an expensive six- or eight-week modeling class. Part of the class required you to also pay for an expensive shoot with a local fashion photographer to build your portfolio. On the day of the shoot, my mom and I showed up with a stack of clothes we pulled from her most fashionable friend's closet and zero idea what to expect. The photographer picked a few looks from the pile and piled on globs of makeup on my face. As she ratted my hair and pinned it up, she casually told my mom that I would probably never book anything in the Salt Lake area. I wasn't "prom queen pretty" enough (ouch). Obviously that was super fun for me to hear right before I stepped in front of her camera. However, she did say that I had a chance at modeling on a larger scale in New York. *New York?* I love New York. And New York is very far away from East High School. That was it. I was sure I had just found the solution to my problems.

As soon as I got home, I started making another list. I found names and phone numbers of modeling agencies in New York City. There were a lot of them, and I had zero fashion background to know which ones were good and which were seedy. *America's Next Top Model* was a huge show at that time. Each season, the winner signed a contract with a different top NY agency. I watched the show religiously, so I decided to write down the names of agencies I had seen on *America's Next Top Model*—IMG, NEXT, Elite, Ford, and few others. I called each agency and found out when they hold their open calls. Back then, agencies used to have a few hours each week where anyone could walk in, have an agent look at you, and then decide if you could be a model. Once again, I presented my findings to my parents and requested we check it out.

Before we go any further, I need to tell you about my parents. These are not the kind of people who aspire to live through their kids. Think of a semi-scary stage mom, then think of the exact opposite. That's my mom. Fashion magazines weren't banned from our house, but I honestly can't remember ever seeing one laying around. Whenever a *Victoria's Secret* catalog came in the mail, I would rush to save the "free pair of undies" card from the back before my Dad tore the magazine in two and put in the outside trashcan. I like to tease my mom that she gave me a bowl cut till I was fourteen . . . which is a bit of a stretch, but I had one for a looong time.

Growing up, we were left to make our own clothing choices and navigate the world of makeup solo. Needless to say, there were some really rough-looking days in my early years with *lots* of smudgy black eyeliner and lopsided ponytails. Once, my sisters and I were looking at pictures of our tween years. In between our laughing and tears, we asked our mom why she didn't swoop in and help us look better. She calmly and wisely responded, "I didn't want my five girls to think their value was in how they looked." I will always respect my mom for her maturity as such a young mom. It would have been easy for her to obsess over our appearances. Surely, she would have received a lot of praise and attention for how cute her five matching little girls were. Despite the constant onslaught of messaging and pressure from the world, my mom did her very best to raise us to understand that our value was found in our minds and hearts, not our looks. Knowing this,

I hope you can see how having a daughter be a model and make money off her body was something my parents never considered.

Potentially, the only thing worse in their minds was what my mom called my "small dog quality." When I set my mind on wanting something, I would yip and bite at her ankles till I got it. After observing that my mind was set on this idea—and after a lot of prayer—my parents got behind me. The week before Thanksgiving of my junior year, I went with my mom on a business trip to New York. In between the appointments with interior design vendors, we met with model agencies. You can only imagine how much faith this required from my parents every step of the way. Spoiler alert: I signed a three-year contract with Elite Model Management. I want to write that this quick trip ended up changing my life, but in truth, I don't think it did. I think this was always part of God's plan. In fact, that was the only reason why my parents let me sign the contract in the first place. Through fasting and prayer, my parents expressed their concerns to God. Modeling was not in their plan for their daughter. However, they both felt that it somehow was in God's plan for His daughter. They told me to fast and pray too. I said a few prayers, but they were mostly along the lines of "This is so cool! Heavenly Father, you're so cool for making this happen. I'm going to be famous!"

After meeting with all the agencies, my mom and I decided to go with Elite for a few reasons:

1. There was an LDS intern from Connecticut. He was a nice kid in his early twenties. He met with us first, took one look at my fancy portfolio from Utah, and politely said, "Never show this to anyone again." He called a few photographers and set me up with a couple of quick shoots. He knew the main agents would want to see some really good photos if they were going to offer me a contract.

2. When we met with the agents, they were good humans. Roman Young, Karen Lee Grybowski, and Jose Covarrubias were angels disguised in chic all-black outfits.

These three sat down with my mom and I and gave us our intro to the high-fashion industry. They also listened patiently as we explained to them how I, because of my faith, would differ from the majority of the models they worked with. We knew that the majority of shoots I would be involved in would not be "For the Strength of Youth" approved. There would be no khakis. Just as a gymnast or ballerina spends her professional hours in a leotard or swimsuit, I, too, would have a unique job uniform. That being said, my parents and agents helped me set some hard boundaries to guide my career:

- No nude
- No semi-nude
- No sheer clothing
- No cigarettes
- No alcohol

At the end of the meeting, Roman, the lead agent, handed me a contract and said, "Congrats. You won the genetic lottery." Everyone laughed and smiled, and then we began preparations for me to move to New York first thing after the new year. "You won the genetic lottery." I couldn't get over that phrase. Overnight, my body went from being the thing that was the focus of bullies and made me miserable to the thing that got me a modeling contract with one of the top agencies in the world and made me money. It was enough to make any sixteen-year-old's head spin.

Over the next five or so weeks, I thought of little else than my new adventure and life. My dad made arrangements for me to transfer to an online high school so I could continue my education while working abroad. My mom coordinated with a family from our old ward in New York for me to stay with for my first couple of weeks so I could still be somewhere familiar. Once I got my feet under me, I would move to the city and live in the Elite model apartment. The logistics of the whole thing weren't that concerning to me. I basically just dreamed of photoshoots, exotic locations, runways, and all that I *knew* God wanted for me. My life was about to start.

I've seen my Heavenly Parents' influence in my life time and time again. I've been blessed by times that I've felt Them nudge me in a direction. In my younger years, I developed that habit of feeling these nudges to take a certain step, and then interpreting where that step and the following steps would lead me. Surely, if God wants me to be a model, He wants me to be famous. Like, no questions asked. This was all part of *His* plan. But I wasn't going to be just famous, I was going to be a good example. I was going to choose the right and be a good model Mormon girl, and I was *for sure* going to be on the cover of the *New Era*. All the boys at East High School were going to seriously regret not dating me, poor suckers. All felt right in the world. Happiness was just a few days and a plane trip to NY away. Dreams are so good and positive thoughts are better. But the danger in interpreting God's nudges is that His end goal or purpose is likely different from what we expect. If we aren't able to separate the heavenly nudge from the earthly interpretation, then we run the risk of ending up right where He wants us, but feeling confused or even bitter because it's different from our personal plan.

It has been over ten years since I signed that contract, and TBH, I'm still learning why God nudged me in the modeling direction. And that's okay. In fact, it's kinda rad. If everything about modeling made sense when I was eighteen years old, there would little to no reason for me to spend any significant amount of time thinking about it. Luckily, so much of my experience made *zero* sense to me, and, in turn, I have spent countless hours thinking about the events, purposes, and effects of my life as a model Mormon.

Chapter 3

Learning How to Walk
. . . in Stilettos

Just off the corner of Third Avenue and Forty-Eighth Street, there is a simple whitewashed brownstone. The Elite Model Management model apartment. There is no special sign or plaque that says, "Teen Tyra lived here"—just a well-worn doorknob and faulty callbox. On the ground floor of the home was Karen Lee's apartment. Karen Lee is an industry scouting legend, but more importantly she is a strong and gentle soul keeping an eye on the endless comings and goings of young girls working in the big city. During my first winter in New York, the city was pummeled by a record-breaking snowstorm. When a thick heap of snow fell on the city in the afternoon, it was like a blanket came down and everyone was tucked into bed. The streets were quiet, and restaurants and businesses shut down early. For a moment, the city that never sleeps was a quiet sleeping beauty. Models spend so much of their time on the run that very rarely are they eating at home. Meals were always on the go, between casting or lipstick touchups on shoots. The snow provided a peaceful evening free of castings or appointments, but it was slightly problematic because we were all hungry and without food. That evening, Karen Lee came to our rescue. She prepared a full meal for us from scratch—something most of us had gone weeks without. I'll never forget how cozy it was to curl up on the sofa with my new roommates eating a plate of homemade eggplant parmesan. It was in moments like this that it was easier to remember that even though we were living on our own in a big city far from home and working all day with adults, we really were just kids.

Another reminder of our youth in the model apartment was the sleeping situation. Think of the model apartments you've seen on *American's Next Top Model*. They had spacious bedrooms with décor and paint colors that made it look like an extension of the Google HQ campus. It was nothing like that. As soon as you entered the building, you climbed a steep narrow staircase—which was fine because we were all so skinny, but problematic because it very difficult to get a decent suitcase up. At the top of the stairs, the space opened up to a sweet living space. The living room was nothing fancy: just a couple of Ikea couches with twisted slip covers, an armchair, and a TV. The glass coffee table was usually covered in obscure and artsy fashion magazines and coffee mugs. There was a small table shoved against the wall where you could often find one model flipping through a magazine looking for her tear sheets and another flipping through a textbook looking for her answer to problem 13 on her homework assignment. The kitchen was tiny. Like, only two people could be in there at once tiny, but that's okay because we were all tiny humans and, as mentioned earlier, food was rarely prepared there.

On the same level in the back, there was a typical New York closet bathroom (conveniently designed to enable you to wash your hands while sitting on the toilet) and a closet bedroom. This bedroom literally only fit a twin mattress and nothing else and was the favorite of veterans of the home. Up another flight of stairs were two more bedrooms and a bathroom. Each of these bedrooms had a dresser, two sets of bunk beds, and a radiator that would creak and steam in the chilly winter months. The life of a model is always up in the air. Literally. When you need to be in Morocco on Wednesday for a swimwear shoot on Thursday, Paris for a fragrance shoot on Sunday, and back in New York for castings on Tuesday, you don't exactly get the luxury of unpacking and using a dresser. I on the other hand, stayed put in New York for my first few months. I unpacked my suitcases and tucked them under my bed. I tucked a few photos I had brought from home into the frame of a large NYC cityscape print that sat on the dresser. Up another flight of stairs was the final level. This level had two bedrooms and a bathroom, but these bedrooms only had two twin beds in each, rather than bunk beds. The rumor was if there were more than thirteen unrelated women living in one home, it was considered a brothel. The top rooms were usually taken by girls who would be staying in the apartment for an extended period, more than a few nights. With so many girls coming and going who just needed a place to crash while in town for a shoot or show season, it was rare to have the same four girls sleeping in one of the bunk beds rooms for more than a couple of nights in a row.

If you were in one of the bunk beds rooms, you got really good at sleeping through the sound of suitcase wheels and zippers at 2 a.m. and communicating with someone without a shared language. I lived with models from all over Brazil, Hungary, Bulgaria, the UK, Virginia, Slovakia, the Czech Republic, Russia, Australia, Argentina, Cuba, Canada, and you get the point. The Elite model apartment was like the freaking United Nations. A very skinny, pretty, and young United Nations. Even though we came from all over the world for only brief intersections, there was a shared sense of community and support. Veteran models would help green models map out their casting or give wardrobe recommendations. "Oh. You're meeting with Marc Jacobs tomorrow? Wear some ripped jeans and a black T. Here, use my black leather purse too."

Considering how young we all were, the majority of us being between fifteen and nineteen years old, it is amazing there weren't more problems. I can't speak for every model apartment, but in ours at the time, there was a real sense of camaraderie. We took care of each other. Each night, the agency faxed (yes, *faxed*) over each model's casting list for the next day. The pages were covered in client names, addresses, contact info, and specific times windows that we were expected to arrive in. Planning the coming day was like putting together a puzzle. The girls who were more familiar with the city helped the new girls find and map out their castings. Sometimes, girls would meet up if they had overlapping castings—sitting in a long line of strangers is a lot easier with a friend. I always felt like I was welcome to join the other models on weekend outings or late dinners after castings. Although (like any other group of random strangers) there were always rude or less-friendly models, I got along with and genuinely liked most models I met. After walking in the Twinkle by Wenlan runway show with

Miranda Kerr, we realized that we were both headed to the same casting. She was a true angel and invited me to hitch a ride across town with her and her driver.

"I don't feel so bad about being tall. I'm not a freak anymore!" was one of the first things I told my mom after moving into the model apartment. Models! They're just like me! They came from all over the world and had strikingly different features, but they all had legs like newborn Bambi. However, I felt like the only one walking like Bambi in my brand-new heels.

There was one night that I remember feeling like I truly, for the first time, belonged. Yulia, a blonde Brit, was snuggled into the corner of a sofa with her legs tucked underneath her. She wore baggy sweats that were rolled at her arm and ankles and balanced a full bowl of fruit on her lap. (Pro tip: When your clothes are too short, you can roll them once and make the shortage look intentional.) I've never met anyone who loved fruit like that girl. Coco Rocha, whose career was about to skyrocket her into modern-day supermodel status, kneeled at the edge of the coffee table and carefully glued pink rhinestones to her Blackberry while gushing about meeting Miss J. Alexander at Starbucks that afternoon. Darla, a dark-featured little brunette from Oregon who could charm strangers at a rate that would impress golden retriever puppies, was there too. For a moment, hundreds of miles away from school and my family, I felt at home.

To this day, nothing feels quite as homey to me as the smell of the NYC subway. Go ahead, judge me. For me, there are few things that make me happier than walking and walking and walking all over New York. Whenever I visit New York City, I plan an afternoon where I can just walk. It doesn't take me long to find myself in an area where I had a casting or shoot so many years before. Running from casting to casting, I became so familiar with those streets. I always knew where the closest Gray's Papaya was, and I more than once showed up to a casting with mustard on my face.

When weather permitted, one of my favorite things to do was to arrange my day so I could finish as close to Battery Park as possible. Battery Park is a long thin park that's mostly a walkway wrapping around the bottom tip of Manhattan Island. In the evening, the park is often full of runners, bladers, kids on little bikes, and couples walking hand in hand. I had a favorite bench with a beautiful view of the Statue of Liberty where I would sit and read for hours. Sometimes I would stop at John's Pizza on Bleeker—the best pizza in NYC no matter what *anyone* tells you—and pick up a pie to enjoy on my bench. John's doesn't do slices, so I would eat what I could of the pie and then give the rest to someone who looked like they were experiencing homelessness and could use a hot slice or two.

Over the next two years, I found myself living in model apartments in Singapore, Milan, and Tokyo. I have so many fond memories of discovering these new foreign cities with my roommates and friends from all over the globe. Probably because we had so much in common culturally, I usually got along fairly well with the Canadians. The Brazilians would do just about anything for you, from making green smoothies "guaranteed" to cure cancer to screaming in the face of aggressive men on the subway. The eastern Europeans were either meek and gentle hearts or fierce forces to reckon with. The model lifestyle is highly transient by nature, so there was often a new friend to visit the sites with after castings.

In Milan, I lived in a model apartment that the agency had split into three mini apartments. I shared a tiny apartment with an angel from Canada named Jenica. We could get from our bunk bed to the bathroom or kitchen in one model stride. We stayed up late watching *Lost* episodes while making magazine cutout collages. Next door there were five sweet Slovakians who often shared their cabbage porridge with me while having me repeat what were likely Slovak curse words. It was also in this apartment, at the table with four Slovakians teens who barely spoke any English, that I had one of the most spiritual experiences of my life. It was here that I first tried Nutella—a moment I will truly never forget.

The third apartment was more transient. Girls were always coming and going. These girls were typically flying into Milan for just a few days for specific shoots while the rest of us were staying in the market to work for several companies for an extended period of time.

I was only in Milan for a month, but it was a pretty happy phase despite a rough start. About four weeks before I left for Milan, I had my wisdom teeth removed. The day of my flight, I woke up with slight pain in the back of my mouth. During the flight overseas, I felt the pain only increase. By my third day in Milan, my entire side of my face was swollen and painful to the touch . . . which is kind of problematic for a model. Nervous, I approached my Milan agency and asked for help. They quickly arranged an appointment for me with an Italian dentist. When I arrived at the dental office, I did my best to explain about my recent wisdom teeth removals and where the pain was coming from using hand motions only because I didn't speak a lick of Italian and no one in the dental office spoke a lick of English. Google Translate! Where were you when I needed you?

The dentist had me lay back in the chair while he filled up large syringe tube of bright-blue goop. He then, using so much force that his muscles were flexed, slowly pushed the whole tube of goop into my infected wisdom tooth socket. I don't know where it all went or how my jaw didn't snap off, but it was the most painful thing I have ever experienced in my entire life.

The room spun around me as my eyes fogged over with tears. A sweet dental hygienist held my hand as I winced in pain through the process. Once the tube was emptied, the dentist handed me a prescription and sent me out the door. I walked about a mile from the dentist back to the train station, concerned that I may pass out every step of the way. I held my face for the thirty-minute metro ride because every bump made my jaw feel like it was going to fall off.

When I finally got to my station, as much as I wanted to curl up in bed, I knew I needed to find the pharmacy. I knew I remembered seeing the green neon cross symbol used on pharmacies somewhere nearby, so I began wandering. I was so out of it, I wandered blocks past the pharmacy basically kitty-corner from the metro station, which I only saw once I gave up and headed back toward my apartment.

I stepped inside and made eye contact with the pharmacist at the end of a long isle of Band-Aids and aspirin bottles. The pharmacist went white, and his eyes got real wide as I walked toward him. I leaned on his counter for support and slid the prescription over the glass top to him. He quickly filled my order and did his best to ask me if I was okay. Unable to speak, I tried to motion to him "how much?" He promptly shook his head and waved me out the door. This was a kind act from a stranger that I hope I will one day get to thank him for.

Once I got to the apartment, unable to read the Italian dosage instructions, I took three of the pills and then slept for the rest of the day and through the night. I was a little sore the next day, but whatever the blue gloop and prescription were, they did the trick.

I, for whatever reason, didn't have much luck in the Milan market. When I say, "didn't have much luck," I mean I didn't book a single job. Day in and day out for four weeks, I ran around the city for castings and then would spend the afternoon and evenings adventuring. Sometimes I was accompanied by another model for an adventure, but often I was by myself. One of my very favorite spots was the Duomo. The quiet of the church reminded me of the huge cathedrals in New York City my parents introduced my sisters and me to when we were kids and that I would duck into during rainstorms when headed to and from castings. The main portion of the cathedral is lined by glass caskets of saint, their skeletons adorned in velvet robes and jewels. One day, I wandered past some velvet ropes when no one was around. When I found myself in a small room with a glass casket, I leaned in close for better look. When I realized I could see the skin on this person's neck between a silver mask and the crimson velvet collar of his robes, I promptly panicked and scurried back to the public areas.

I guess I was a pretty typical teen in the sense that I felt quite invisible and a little above the law. Da Vinci's *The Last Supper*, a fifteenth-century fresco mural, is on the original crumbling wall with a protective museum built around it. The museum allows a few people to view the piece for limited amounts of time in shifts, and photos are strictly forbidden. When an agency employee saw the picture I snuck with my flash covered, he told me to never show anyone the photo again because I could go to jail. Whether that is true or not, I believed him.

Though most of our castings were just a metro, tram, or bus ride away, the agency employed a driver, Giuseppe, to help us to get to castings that were beyond the public transit systems. When Giuseppe—we called him Bocha, and he called us his little sisters—wasn't driving us to and from castings, he was looking out for us. It was rumored that Bocha had recently been released from jail and had connections with the mafia. Regardless of whether that rumor had any truth to it, if we were seen with Bocha, no one would mess with us.

One of my favorite days in Milan was when Bocha drove us out to Parma—birthplace of parmesan cheese—for a casting. Once the casting was over, we stopped at a beautiful farm in the middle of a vineyard. An employee helped Bocha and the other models to a small wine tasting. It blew my mind when the employee poured a bit of wine into the glass to rinse and line the glass and then dumped the wine on the ground. Only then was the glass properly treated for the actual wine tasting. After Bocha had a few glasses, I made a nervous joke about him needing to be sober enough to drive us home. He laughed and explained that he has been drinking wine like water since he was a child. I bought a massive wedge of aged parmesan while Bocha shoved three or four into his coat. I had complete intentions to eat the wedge over the next few days, but it was gone by the time we returned to Milan.

Jenica and I often met up for lunch at a fancy restaurant just outside of our apartment called Noy. Noy was the kind of place that had fresh white tablecloths and water with or without bubbles. Dim lighting and tables illuminated by candles gave the restaurant a cozy, sleepy feeling even when the sun was blaring outside. Much to our pleasure, Noy let us and other local models eat lunch free. Apparently, the benefits of filling your lunch tables with pretty young women outweighed the cost of salad bar salads (which didn't appreciate ranch dressing). Just a good old "you scratch my back, I'll scratch yours" situation. This kind of setup was fairly common in the model life. Nearly every night, the landline in the New York model apartment would start ringing around 7 p.m. On one of first nights in the apartment, I was home alone. I was on my bunk bed planning my route all over the city to hit up all of my castings for the next day. When the phone rang, I came crashing down the stairs, worried it may be an agent trying to reach me.

"Hello, this is Rosie."

"ROOOOOOOOsie. My beautiful baby. How are you?"

"Good . . . ?"

"Rosie, baby, what time can I come pick you up tonight?"

"I'm sorry . . . who is this?"

"Rosie, sweetheart, it's Fredrico! I'm going to take my baby girl out tonight. Be ready at eight?"

"Do I know you?"

"Baby, I know all of the girls. They're my best friends. Make me happy tonight and be ready by eight. Okay, babe?"

We went back and forth a few times until another model came home. She quietly observed our conversation for a moment and then walked over to me, took the receiver from my hand and hung it up.

"Club PR promoters," she explained, "If you want a free night out on the town, you can go with them. You'll have all the free drinks you could want and sit in the VIP section, but you'll also wake up looking wasted for your morning castings. If you go to the right clubs, you can make a deal with that bar where they'll give you half the cut if you can get one of the investment banker dudes to buy you the most expensive bottle of champagne." I may not be able to do a cartwheel, but at least I've known how to con shady dudes in da club since I was sixteen.

These promoters called nearly every night from the swankiest clubs in New York trying to lure young girls into their dark limos. The agency would routinely change the landline number to deter them. But like the native New York rat, they always found a way in where they weren't wanted. When their invitations were accepted, which thanks to the constant turnover of models, seemed often, they would pick girls up, take them to dinner at the fanciest restaurants, and then take them to the VIP sections of their clubs till the early morning. All of this would be pretty rad if you were at least twenty-one years old with your friends on a weekend night. Unfortunately, most of these girls were underage teenagers who spoke limited English and needed to be awake and fresh for 8 a.m. shoots.

I'll admit that there were times that I wished I was brave enough to tag along. I also wish I could say I didn't go because I was focused on my studies or something valiant like that. The truth is I was scared. Yes, scared of the horror stories I heard in health class about date rape drugs, but mostly just scared of not being a good Mormon girl. I know lots of people may look down on me for having such a naive motivation, but guess what? I was sixteen and my naïveté protected me. Yes, to this day, I'm still sad I missed meeting Mary Kate and Ashley at Vin Diesel's birthday party with my roomies. However, I'm not sad a client never fired me last minute because I showed up to a shoot with bags under bloodshot eyes. Did many girls go clubbing without serious repercussions? Yes. Did I also know of a girl who woke up in a hotel room alone, totally naked, and without a piece of clothing or phone anywhere to be found in the room? Yes. In this type of situation, I'll take the regret of missing out over the potential regret of going out, any day.

After lunch at Noy, Jenica and I would part ways for the afternoon. She usually had a shoot, and I had castings. We promised each other we would only get gelato once each day. If we did something really special or brave that day, like yell back at the leering Italian men on the street or make a new friend while sitting in the cattle call line of models, we could get it twice. But we had to wait for the other one to get home and go together. The unusually warm November weather made perfect conditions for late-night strolls through the dreamy cobblestone streets to our favorite gelato shop, Chocolat. My favorite flavor was the creamiest vanilla bean with Nutella ribbons folded in served with a pure chocolate spoon. The fact that euros look like quarters also helped jack up the frequency of our gelato runs.

Sure, I missed out on some classic American teen experiences, but no one feels bad for me when they hear I spent $600 USD in four weeks on gelato. Milan beats prom . . . for me at least. Looking back, I can see that my progression in high school, because of my limited understanding and struggles, was stuck. I needed something different. Living and working in New York, Italy, Singapore, and Tokyo provided the priceless education that shaped who I am today with the help of many positive experiences and relationships. Of course, there were some tough experiences too.

In Singapore, the model apartment housed men and women. When I landed in the tiny island nation of Singapore, it was pitch black and a zillion degrees outside. I was sixteen and out of the US for the very first time and feeling very alone. It was the middle of the night when I hailed a cab from the curb of the airport. I tried to relax by focusing on the wooden beads hanging from the rearview mirror. The cab smelled like a sweaty man body mixed with incense, so I rolled down my window, closed my eyes, and let the hot tropical air blow on my face. I gave up trying to find my zen when the cab driver got mad and rolled my window up. Turning on the child lock was a nice touch. The heat and my anxiety pressed down on me as I lugged the suitcase that I would live out of for three months up the apartment complex driveway. I noticed little lizards scurrying on the ground through the weak glow of the street lamps on the black road. When I finally got up to the apartment, the Singaporean agency employee who lived in and managed the model apartment sleepily greeted me and led me to my room. It was nearly pitch black inside, but I could make out one large queen-sized bed and two twins. The queen bed's covers looked . . . lived in . . . and I could make out a figure sleeping in one of the twins. The host gestured to the empty twin in the corner. I awkwardly tried to lift my huge suitcase over to the bed without making too much noise. Before I reached my bed for the next three months, the man crashed into the queen bed. Too scared to ask where the bathroom was so I could brush my teeth or change into pajamas, I curled up on top of the bed and tried to cover my face with the thin sheet. I was too overwhelmed to cry. I kept thinking, *How did I get here?* Just a few short months ago, I was a Mia Maid in Salt Lake City. Now I was a model in a room with two strangers, and one of them was a dude! Well, both were dudes. I just didn't know that yet.

In the morning, I timidly walked out of the bedroom to find my saving grace, Michelle. Michelle is a meek and stunning Canadian who I lived with for a bit in New York. When my agency was making arrangements for my Singapore stay, I was relieved to hear that Michelle would be there at the same time. Michelle could clearly see how unsettled I was. She took me into her room, closed the door, and gave me a crash course on my new Singaporean life. With a worn map spread out on the bed, Michelle helped me navigate the nuances of the metro and bus systems. She drew little hearts around our apartment location and then a star on our agency's coordinates. She told me where to get a cell phone and gave me a rundown of the Singaporean laws that I needed to make sure I followed. Mainly no jaywalking and no spitting gum (gum that I brought into the country because you can't buy gum in Singapore) or really anything out.

On one particularly frustrating Singapore day, I was feeling real rebellious and jaywalked in front of my apartment. Just my luck, a cop drove by at that exact moment. He slowed his car to a crawl and rolled down his window. I froze dead in my tracks. With his arm extended out the car window, he pointed his finger right at me as he drove by. I nearly crapped my pants right then and there. Singapore doesn't mess around with their laws and punishment. A couple of kids got caned the day I arrived because they were caught tagging a wall.

Singapore was a really hard phase for me. I didn't feel like the agency there was excited about me, and I sure as heck wasn't excited about them. Life in the model apartment wasn't working out well either. One night, I was scared awake by the sound of my second roommate, a male model from Australia, crashing into our room. The apartment host was out for the night, so it was just us in the room, and he was drunk. And when I say "drunk," I mean *druuuuunk*. He tripped over his guitar and smashed into his bed and end table. The sound of his guitar slamming against the tile floor was so loud I was sure he was going to wake up our whole neighborhood. I hadn't spent much time around drunk people before, and I was terrified. Making his way to the attached bathroom, he threw up on the floor and then proceeded to wretch into the toilet. Just like every bad scary movie scene, I peeked from underneath my sheet to see his dark figure approaching my bed. The glow from the bathroom bit lit his silhouette which made it extra freaky when he mumbled my name. I wanted to run out of the room screaming, but I couldn't move. There are very few times in my life that I feel like I have received specific and immediate instructions from heaven, but this was one of those times. "Play dead" came clear and urgent into my mind. I froze and closed my eyes right as he leaned over my body. His hot sick breath engulfed my face as he screamed my name inches above me. "Play dead." I was still as a corpse, but all of my senses were firing on high alert. Surely this feral animal would be able to detect my pounding heartbeat. Twelve years later, I still get upset telling this story. Who knows what could have happened that night. In the morning, I called my parents and cried my eyes out. Naturally, they called my New York agents in a rage. My New York agents then called my Singaporean agents in a rage. Then my Singapore agents called me in a rage. If my Singaporean agents weren't huge Rosie fans before, they for sure weren't now. They were livid that I hadn't called them first, but more than anything, they shredded me for telling my parents and NY agents. In a culture where saving face is *everything*, I was guilty of tarnishing their reputation. They weren't mad at the twenty-four-year-old model who was dangerously and violently drunk yelling over the bed of a sixteen-year-old—they were mad at the six-teen-year-old for telling her mom.

If you—actually, sadly—*when* you experience any kind of assault or harassment, don't let the fear of getting in trouble, embarrassment, or really anything stop you from telling someone. When I was a kid, my mom would make my sisters and I listen to these cassette tapes called "Safety Kids." Safety Kids was a compilation of songs, sung by kids, about how to react in tricky situations. After all these years, I can still remember some of the lyrics. "Sometimes you just got to yell and scream. Sometimes it's the only thing to do. Noisy as a firetruck, you just gotta open up." Be loud like a firetruck. Let it out. Find someone you love and trust and share your story. If that person reacts poorly, I need to you build up your courage and tell someone else. You need an ally.

After my roommate's drunken night and a morning of getting in trouble for saying something about it, I no longer cared. I was pain-fully homesick, heat sick, and just all around sick of Singapore. I was sick of the rules, the unrelenting hellish heat and humidity that would make me sweat from my kneecaps, my smoking roommates and their obsession with Asian horror films. Needless to say, on a scale from one to hangry infant, I was an eleven on the fussy scale. (Note: I have since been back to Singapore and absolutely love the country. It is a beauti-ful, clean, food utopia that my tummy misses regularly.) Sure, we can all look back at fussy-pants Rosie and want to give her a good shake. "Open your eyes! You're living on an island in southeast Asia! Go have some adventures! Snap out of it!"

Near the end of my stay in Singapore, I was on the short list of a group of models who would fly to Thailand for a runway show. I called my NY agent and asked them to make sure I didn't have to go because I wanted to try to make it home for prom. I swear I could hear his eyes roll through the phone. In my defense, I didn't really know how magical Thailand was because this is pre-Instagram life, but still it just shows how extremely anxious I was to get back to the States.

Much to my relief at the time and my present regret, I didn't make the cut for the Thailand show. I made it home in time for prom. Luckily, I didn't need to stress about what to wear. I worked several times with Jill Stuart, so I had a couple of beautiful dresses to choose from.

As much as I loved living and working abroad, New York and I understood each other. When I first landed in New York, I had couple of pairs of ill-fitting American Eagle jeans, some worn printed Ts from places like In-N-Out and a taco shop in San Diego, and pink-and-white Puma sneakers. Kate, an agency employee in her twenties, stayed late one night to help me go shopping. She wore all black and made shopping vintage sound cool before it was. She was kind but firm and direct in a way that made me hesitate before responding to any of her quick questions. It was drizzling when our cab pulled up to the New York flagship Diesel store. As we walked up the damp sidewalk, I noticed the store seemed closed which really shouldn't have been a surprise considering how late it was. I hesitated. Kate, the overwhelming, cool New Yorker tasked with the difficult job of making this poor little Utah girl look less . . . Utah, brushed past me and said, "I called them and told them I was coming in with one of our top models." She reached the large double doors quickly. A store employee appeared and began unlocking the door from the inside. Just before he pushed the door open to us, Kate looked back at me and, in both a plea and command, said, "Try to look confident." As we entered the store, an employee appeared with jeans Kate had apparently requested when she called earlier. I was whisked into a dressing room before any of the employees could get a good look at me and realize I was nobody worth staying late for. Kate shoved a pair of black-washed skinny jeans over the dressing room door with a "try these quick." They were tighter than skin tight. I had to pull at the waist band with all my might to button them. "They work?" Kate asked through the curtain. She was just as eager as all the other employee presently waiting on me to get out of there. "Yeah, sure!" I said, too nervous to ask for a bigger size. "Good. Let's go."

I wore those jeans and a pair of gray knock-off Converse day in and day out as I walked the streets of New York. From the model apartment, to casting, to shoots, to go-sees. It was just me, my "model uniform," and the city streets. When I'd reach a casting, I'd slip out of my Converse, slide them into my bag, and step into my hot-pink heels. My agent, Roman, gave me this very first pair of heels. The heel was a shiny hot pink, but the foot of the shoe was a pink tweed—horrible now, but I was very into it at the time—with a shiny hot-pink button on the toe.

Sometimes I try to remember what I was wearing when I met Anna Wintour and shudder at the likelihood that I was proudly wearing my pink tweed heels like they were right off the runway. I only made it to the *Vogue* offices in the famed *Condé Naste* building, essentially the Holy of Holies of the industry, a handful of times. I sat on a white pleather chair, crammed next to the desk of one of the *Vogue* editors while she flipped through my book. Every inch of wall and surface had a photograph or torn portion of a magazine page taped to it. That place looked like a middle school magazine collage maker went hog wild in there. I snapped out of my zone-out when I heard the editor ask, "Are you ready to meet Anna?" Her eyes locked mine like she was trying to get some kind of confirmation from me that I wasn't going to do anything stupid or make her look bad. Having zero idea who "Anna" was, I quickly nodded my head. She took in a deep breath and was down the hall before she exhaled. I sprang to my feet to follow her, catching up right before she made a sharp left turn in to a large office. She exchanged a few words with a woman behind a desk regarding an upcoming shoot. I stood just beyond the doorway and surveyed my surroundings. The editor then brought me a pair of heels from the desk and instructed me to put them on. I did my best to quickly maneuver the complicated and intricate lace fronts while ogling the hot-pink rhinestone-covered heels. As soon as I was laced in, I took a few steps toward the two at the desk. With both of their eyes locked on the shoes, the "Anna" character instructed me to profile to her with one foot in front of the other and knees slightly bent. I did as she directed, and then I was ushered out.

A few weeks later, I found myself in an old movie theater for a photoshoot. I can't speak for anyone else's career, but for the vast majority of the shoots I did, I had zero idea what they were for while shooting. I once shot the cover of *Women's Wear Daily*, but I only knew when the receptionist for a casting I was at held up that day's WWD with my face on the cover and asked, "Is this you?" This movie theater shoot was no different. I knew it was a little higher scale than my typical job because there was a folding table with a black velvet tablecloth covered in jewels that had its own security guard. Too scared to ask too many questions, I just showed up and sat in the makeup chair when they asked me to. Much to my surprise, they started to apply makeup to my legs rather than my face. I distinctly remember wishing I would have shaved my legs that day. It all came together when a dresser helped me put on those familiar pink-bedazzled heels that probably deserved their own security guard. A couple months later, back home for Christmas in Utah, I checked the 2006 December *Vogue* and found a full-page photo of my legs. The rest of the photos in the story featured a big-name model and her son, but apparently, she couldn't fit the heels for that shot, so they needed me and my small feet. My model friends, many whose actual faces were regularly in *Vogue*, would later tease me that people were going to stop me on the street because they recognized my legs.

Over the course of my brief two-year career, I was extremely blessed to work with inspiring and talented people. Though at the time I didn't fully appreciate how privileged I was to have my makeup done by Pat McGrath or to be styled by Patti Wilson, I felt a sense of respect for the skill and craft and enjoyed working with them. Between working with both big-name and lesser-known powerhouses, incredible agents, and kind model friends, I was blessed by many in the industry.

One particular duo played an immensely important part of my life: my main agent, Roman, and his boyfriend, Damon Rutland. First of all, they're the most beautiful couple in the whole world, and you need to google them and see for yourself. Phew. I just had to get that off my chest. Second, more impressive than their beautiful skin and perfect bone structure are their hearts. When the $2,000 monthly rent at the model apartment was too expensive for me, these angel men took little Mormon me in and let me live on their couch for *months*. They would take me out to brunch and invite me to dine with them and their friends on the weekends. Living with a gay couple at seventeen was a unique experience that I considered designed by God. I feel privileged to have been blessed by the good example of these men. They loved and cared for each other and the people around them. They opened my eyes to what it did and didn't mean to be gay and I will always be grateful for the kindness they showed and continue to show me.

Probably one of the most important lessons I learned from modeling was from Roman and Damon. Each morning, I would make my little couch bed and read from the Book of Mormon. One lazy Sunday afternoon, Roman asked me what the Church's stance was on gays. My mind raced as I tried to figure out how to answer. I stumbled through some awkward and painful sentences, and then ended with, "I don't really know. But I know you guys are really good people." I was young, and though my mom had a good friend from FIT who was gay, homosexuality wasn't something we had really talked about. I knew it wasn't "kosher" within the Church, but I didn't know how to reconcile the Church policy, whatever it was, and the loving human who let me crash on his couch for three months.

Roman graciously shared his story and experience growing up gay and coming out. He told me stories about the harassment and abuse he endured in college. As he shared some highs and lows, I came to understand the Roman was exactly as God intended him to be.

I encourage all Mormons to sit down and have a conversation with someone who is gay, especially a gay member of the Church. Scratch that. Make it a *listen*, not a conversation. Just listen to them with an open mind and heart. Love them and listen to them. Hold space for their experience just as you would like someone to do for you. If you are lucky, you will feel the love our Heavenly Parents have for them, just as They have for you. Remember that your baptismal covenant was to "mourn with those that mourn" and to "comfort those that stand in need of comfort" (Mosiah 18:9). We did not covenant to judge when we think we should judge.

What does this have to do with anything? This experience opened my eyes to what eventually became a foundational principle to my life. I can and should learn from people who are different from me. Without knowing it, Roman taught me a valuable lesson that Heavenly Mother and Father love all of Their children. They are working overtime and through the night to help us all get home. It also laid the foundation for my belief that we can find God in all things. Yes, revelation and spiritual lessons can be found in the scriptures, temple, and church, but it is such a blessing that they can also be found in experiences, modern media and literature, and the people around us.

Chapter 4

The Lord Looketh on the Heart

I fear that sharing negative elements of my career may give the impression that the industry is full of lurking dark creatures more concerned about the September issue than the soul of an individual or that every day during my modeling career was dark and painful. There were so many good days, good experiences, and good people during this phase of life.

Traveling the world at such a young age introduced me to people and places many will never get to enjoy. Booking a big show or job was always an honor and so exciting. For a girl who rarely "made the cut" in high school, this was huge. Runway shows with their makeup, fancy clothes, tables of jewelry, bright lights, and loud music felt like dance recitals, and *I loved* them. I always felt honored to observe masters of their craft like Pat McGrath, Zac Posen, and Jill Stuart work their magic.

However, I feel it's important that I share some of the very real negative experiences I had to be true to the experience. Especially considering how many, if not most, models could tell similar or worse tales. Yes, I traveled the world. I saw magical places and had exciting stories to share when I went home. But there were also elements I've glossed over when I have shared my story over the last ten years.

Very seldom would I talk about the time I shot outside on a record-shattering cold day in New York wearing a lace tank dress. It was a dark, cloudy day, so the photographer had to shoot with a slow shutter speed. My body shook so violently that I had to brace myself by grip-ping the frozen bars of the old fire escape on the side of the building because I was blurring the shots. The frozen bars left burns down my palms like I had been struck with a ruler. The final photo is a close-up. You couldn't even tell I was outside or on a cool-looking fire escape.

Or there's the winter-wear shoots in the dead of summer on the flat rooftops of Brooklyn. One shoot started early in the morning and shot well into the night. The shoot was on a tight budget, so they didn't provide lunch. They rolled their eyes when I asked for a glass of water while standing in the blazing heat for hours because the makeup artist would need to touch up my lipstick. When the shoot wrapped around 2 a.m., I, a sixteen-year-old girl, walked alone through Brooklyn, which wasn't the hipster mecca it is today, to the nearest subway station. As I look back, I could punch myself for not calling a cab, but I also wonder what in the world those adults could have been thinking sending me out at 2 a.m. alone.

The ugly truth about the prettiest industry is that at its bare bones, the fashion industry profits off little girls playing an adult game. I, like so many of my fellow models, was young and eager to please. I wanted to do a good job, and I wanted to be a good model. Saying "no" to a room full of powerful adults was tough. After all, they're the artists. I'm just a prop in their vision. And everyone, myself included, knew that if one prop gives the artist any problems, there's a line of girls in the hall willing to play by whatever rules it takes to work their way to the top. It is a sad reality that many young women agree to participate in inappropriate shoots because they simply don't feel like they have any other option.

As I look back, there are a lot of experiences that I can't believe I actually went through, and there are a fair number of adults I wish I could go back in time and say a few words to. Like the stylist on a shoot who suggested I should only order a salad for lunch because I "had a tummy." (I was seventeen, 103 pounds, and five foot eleven. I ordered a cheeseburger.) Or the photographers who pressured me to take off my clothes for photos and would threaten me with, "Your agents are going to be mad when they hear you wouldn't cooperate," when I would refuse to undress for them.

I could go on and on with examples of sleazy people, usually men, trying to take advantage of and abuse their power. The sad reality is that in these situations, very rarely do models have someone sticking up for them as a human, not just for their career.

A couple of years after I stopped modeling, my mom and I were discussing my experience when the idea of "regret" came up. I triumphantly stated that I didn't regret a single shoot. My mom, totally supportive and proud, lightly said she kinda sorta wished I could take back that "child prostitute shoot."

Record scratch Hold up, Mom.

That child *what* shoot? When the heck did I do a child *prostitute* shoot? My brain raced for any memory of participating in something so disgusting and deplorable. Lovingly, my mom reminded me of the shoot in question.

The shoot took place in a dilapidated motel on Coney Island. The room consisted of four bare and heavily stained twin mattresses stacked two deep and shoved in a corner. There was one bashed-up wooden chair and a dead rat behind the broken radiator. Luckily, someone brought a flat bedsheet to cover the mattresses and create a barrier between me and the cockroaches crawling inside them. The photographer rented the room by the half hour, and there was a communal toilet (no sink) in the hall. I was sixteen years old. Call me naive, but it had never crossed my mind that prostitution motels even existed. I just thought they picked the location because it looked unique.

As the makeup artist rouged my cheeks, I eyed my wardrobe for the shoot. Relief brushed over me when I observed that nothing looked more revealing than a one-piece swimsuit. As the stylist laced up a vintage Dior leotard (read: corset) I slowly shimmied and watched the delicate beaded fringe make light dance on the walls of chipped and faded paint. I felt pretty and happy because I wouldn't have to push back or defend myself today. I could relax and let them pose and coach me. Everyone, from the photographer to the stylist, was super nice, and the shoot went off without a hitch. The thing that felt odd was the crew insisting I rub hand sanitizer all over my body every time I got off the bed or floor.

It wasn't until years later, with the help of my caring mom, that I understood what I was depicting that day. The location, my wardrobe, the way they posed me, and my very apparent age came together in photographs that hypersexualize children. Child prostitution is one of the lowest and most vile institutions on this earth, and at the hands of a room of adults, I, a child, glamorized it. I had studied the children sex slave industry in college, and the realization of this shoot introduced an immense sense of shame and pain into my life for quite some time. Though I was completely innocent in my involvement—involvement that I see as a real form of abuse and exploitation—I felt violated and sick.

With time, therapy, and the Atonement of Jesus Christ, I have found peace, but I think this will always be a sore spot on my soul. Thankfully, Jesus Christ can heal us from wounds that we sustain at the hands of others' poor choices.

Until recently, I have never completely shared this story. Why? Fear and shame. I feared the day that someone would stumble onto the images online and treat me like damaged goods. I feared being seen as hypocritical, imperfect, and a poor example. Looking back now, I understand that I wrongly thought leaders got to the place of leadership by perfection. I don't know about you, but rarely do I learn from or really connect with people who seem to have never made a mistake or had a real trial.

I have a Savior, Jesus Christ, who is a perfect example in all things. He is real good at His job, so I'm not going to try to take His place. I don't know about you, but what I need more of is examples of people who have fallen, sinned, and made mistakes and then moved forward. Everyone can be a good example somehow, but only Christ needs to be the example of perfection.

I'm inspired by the examples of Alma the Elder and Alma the Younger: two really good dudes with really shady pasts. When appropriate, they were open and honest with others about their experiences and the role the Atonement played in helping them become more like Christ. I think it is significant to note how important it was that the people who knew these men during their dark days allowed both Almas to move on from their pasts after they made amends and dealt with the consequences.

Elder Holland taught:

Let people repent. Let people grow. Believe that people can change and improve. Is that faith? Yes! Is that hope? Yes! Is that charity? Yes! Above all, it is charity, the pure love of Christ. If something is buried in the past, leave it buried. . . .

Such dwelling on past lives, including past mistakes, is just not right! It is not the gospel of Jesus Christ. In some ways it is worse than Lot's wife because at least she destroyed only herself. In cases of marriage and family, wards and branches, apartments and neighborhoods, we can end up destroying so many others.[1]

I am not perfect, nor do I have it all figured out, but my hope is that this experience can help someone somehow. Even if it is not readily talked about, there is not a single leader in the Church with a perfect past. The twists and turns in our pasts make them beautiful. In the words of Richard Rohr, "The skater pushing both right and left eventually goes where he or she wants to go."[2]

Consider that some of the most important events in our faith came after some type of a "fall." Eve, and in turn Adam, chose to *fall* so that she could act as a catalyst and initiate the plan of salvation. Jesus Christ was resurrected, and in turn, all of us can be resurrected, because He first sunk to the lowest depths and died for us.

As I look back on this shoot now, I don't feel waves of shame. The thought of someone seeing those pictures doesn't make me want to hide in a cave like it once did. In fact, I like sharing them because they teach a valuable lesson that applies to anyone who has ever taught modesty within the LDS Church.

If modesty was just about girls covering their shoulders, tummies, and upper thighs and wearing one-piece swimsuits, then the shoot in question could have been a *New Era* special on appropriate swimwear.

I hope we can all come to better understand, as is so clearly evident by this photoshoot, that modesty is more than body parts to cover.

Modesty, a principle taught in scripture to both men and women, is a commitment an individual makes privately with his or her Maker. If an individual's modesty, or any private commitment to God, was up for public opinion, we wouldn't wear our garments *underneath* our clothing. Modesty is about who we are as children of Heavenly Parents and how we act accordingly. Modesty is about treating ourselves and others with love and respect. It's having the inner confidence and peace that makes others' gaze and praise of our appearance, status, or possessions unnecessary and unimportant. We are to be modest in word, action, attitude, and outlook. Not just in how we dress.

Modesty is many things, but it is *not* about being "hot." May "modest is hottest" die a peaceful death and drift far away never to be heard from again. Why? Because we aren't fooling anyone, and can we really imagine Heavenly Father teaching His girls that they should be modest so the boys will think they're hot? Definitely not.

When I was in Young Women, a leader told us that if we wore tank tops, we were basically walking pornography. This is gross and a freaking 100 on the creepy shame level. A child's shoulder does not equal pornography. If we are hypersexualizing children, we have far greater issues on our hands than tank tops.

Is there an element of modesty that covers clothing choices? Absolutely. Do I think this one piece of the greater modesty puzzle is deserving of the present amount of air time it gets? Nope.

> The Lord seeth not as man seeth; for man looketh on the outward appearance, but the Lord looketh on the heart. (1 Samuel 16:7)

Let's not shortchange our young women or young men by denying them the opportunity to learn the meat of the doctrine of modesty. If we really believe these are elect spirits reserved for the last days, don't we think they can handle it? Teach them correct principles, and let them govern themselves. Sound familiar?

When I speak to Young Women groups, I never mention what body parts to cover and how much. Today's little women are smart. They are powerful. They are learning and growing disciples of Christ. They, like all of us, need room to safely try things out without being ostracized or shamed.

President Packer taught:

> True doctrine, understood, changes attitudes and behavior.
>   The study of the doctrines of the gospel will improve behavior quicker than a study of behavior will improve behavior. . . . That is why we stress so forcefully the study of the doctrines of the gospel.[3]

Again, our girls are smart. They know the current Church standard for clothing for those who have made covenants. As their personal connection with heaven grows stronger, their commitment to proper clothing choices will follow. And at the end of the day, what is more important that they understand—life-saving gospel doctrines or how to dress like a good Mormon?

I'm not saying we tell the Mia Maid who shows up to mutual in a miniskirt she looks like a total babe. In fact, unless you have a relationship of love and respect with her and are in private, it would be best that you not say anything about her appearance at all. Instead try out, "So glad you are here!" or "That's a really good point you made," or "Wow! You're really good at that."

My experience in understanding the weight of my innocent choice while modeling could only be safely facilitated by my loving mother. Not everyone has that blessing. This guidance may need to come from a loving leader, sister, or friend. Regardless of the trusted role we play in a young woman's life, let's be sure we help her understand what modesty is really about. Help her feel the love of her Savior. It may not happen overnight, but as she comes to understand the love and respect He has for her, she will outgrow anything, from clothing to words to deeds to attitudes that are ill-suited to the queen that she is.

Lastly, as daughters of God, we are all in different phases of our "queen training." However, we all know that lesson one teaches us to love one another, never shame.

And since we're all geared up to kill inappropriate cultural teachings, let's get something else out there. We believe that women will be punished for their own sins, not for men's inappropriate thoughts. Women and men are all accountable for their own actions. Shaming young women, or women of any age, into fitting a dress standard that is far more cultural than doctrinal by making them feel accountable for someone else's choice is flat-out wrong. Not only is it damaging to the women, but it is immensely damaging to the men.

If boys grow up with the constant messaging that they aren't in control of their thoughts or accountable for their actions, what kind of men will that make them? I'll let you answer that, but can we really be surprised when we struggle to have men step up when this is what they're taught? When I hear fathers referred to as "the oldest child in the family" or the "less nurturing parent," my blood boils. It is offensive to them, and it is offensive to Heavenly Father. I dare anyone to say Heavenly Father isn't a nurturing parent or equally contributing spouse.

Heavenly Father and Jesus Christ are the ultimate examples of "real men." What if men thought of being more Christlike when they hear "man up" or "be a man" rather than being an emotional void? Christ cried. A lot! Christ cared for children and the sick. A lot! Christ felt a wide range of emotions openly and encouraged those around Him to too. Christ openly shared His faith. Christ was comfortable asking for help when He felt scared and weak, and He never hesitated to tell people He loved them. By today's standard, Jesus may not be a "man's man," but scout's honor, you won't find a better definition or example of a real man elsewhere.

Men are people too. They feel all the same emotions that women do—fear, excitement, anger, sadness, joy, disappointment, and so on. Unfortunately, our world has feminized certain human emotions, and even more unfortunately, being feminine in our world is seen as "less than." This series of unfortunate events has left our boys and men feeling authentic emotions but having no way to cope with them. Fear, sadness, heartache, and the like get stuffed down, and these poor young men are left with anger, which can easily lead to violence. Our men are hurting, and we are wrong when we don't help them or even let them address it in a healthy manner.

Looking back now, the young man who pinned me to the cafeteria floor and nearly broke my shoulder and arm was probably dealing with some pretty intense emotions—emotions that he only knew how to express through violence. Does this excuse his actions? Heck to the no! But it does make me feel a little more compassion toward him.

Now, I happen to know that this young man grew up and, from his wife's Instagram posts, looks like a sweet husband and dad. That's happy! But not everyone has that happy ending. There is something to be considered when *all* (I know if I say "all," someone will find one contradicting case, but I'm still saying "all") of the horrific shootings in our country are at the hands of men. We are doing something wrong here in how we raise our boys. We need to change.

I look forward to the day when modesty lessons, taught equally amongst women and men, are about humility, living within your means, how we treat others, and the words we use. Which I know sounds buck wild, but considering that's what the scriptures talk about when modesty is mentioned, it might a good adjustment.

Notes

1. Jeffrey R. Holland, "The Best Is Yet to Be," *Ensign*, January 2010.
2. Richard Rohr, *Falling Upward: A Spirituality for the Two Halves of Life* (San Francisco: Jossey-Bass, 2011), 28.
3. Boyd K. Packer, "Little Children," *Ensign*, November 1986.

Chapter 5

New Face

Brand-new models are called "New Faces," and when you're a New Face, nobody knows (read: cares) who you are. You spend a lot of your time running around Manhattan in sneakers and changing into high heels in glossy lobbies before meeting industry influencers like magazine editors, photographers, and casting directors. Your job is to put your best stiletto forward and hope they like you more than the ten plus other waiflike teens they met that morning and invite you to their casting calls. When you're not running between go-sees, you do test shoots. Test shoots are basically collaborations between models, photographers, makeup artists, and designers who are trying to build their portfolios.

On one of my first Sundays in the city, my agents booked me for a test shoot early in the morning. My agents were really good people, and they knew I didn't want to work on Sundays, but they understandably pushed most of the boundaries to see if I would bend some of the rules once I was out of my parents' supervision. More than once they requested that I "put Mormon Rosie on the back burner for just a couple of months." They understandably wanted a little bit of time with a little more freedom to get me jobs with more artistic photographers. "Once you make a name for yourself by shooting with some of the top photographers and designers, you can set your hard boundaries and everyone will have to respect them."

Artistic in the industry is often code for "edgy," and artistic photographers don't like models who set boundaries or limits on their creativity. When you're a model, you're more of a prop in someone's creative vision than a human with feelings and rights.

I sat on a cold orange subway seat and unfolded the piece of paper that my agency had given me with the shoot details. "Call the photographer when you get to X stop. He'll meet you there and walk you to his apartment." His apartment? Meeting some random photographer for shoot in his Brooklyn apartment felt a little shady, but who was I to question them? I naively trusted that I would be totally safe on any shoot my agency booked. Would they knowingly put me in harm's way? Absolutely not. But they also didn't see themselves as my guardians in any shape or form. Hence why no one batted an eye at sending a sixteen-year-old girl to shoot alone with a male photographer in his apartment.

I finally arrived at the proper stop fifteen minutes late thanks to MTA weekend construction. I called the photographer to let him know I was there and then waited alone on a chilly Brooklyn corner. Soon, a man in his twenties wearing ripped black skinny jeans and a puffy coat approached and introduced himself as the photographer. We made small talk as we weaved through the side streets of Brooklyn toward his "studio."

I never hid that I was a Mormon from people I worked with, but I sure as heck didn't lead with it. "I'm a Mormon" wasn't exactly a catchy marketing phrase in 2005, and I didn't feel like it was necessary or normal to bring up one's religious affiliation within the first fifteen minutes of a business interaction. I could still hear the screech of trains coming and going from the station when I felt the distinct impression to tell the photographer that I was a Mormon. With every stride toward his apartment, the impression lingered. I don't remember what he was talking about at that point, but I do know it made absolutely zero sense when I responded with, "Oh cool. Yeah, so I'm a Mormon." The young photographer was a little caught off guard, but he politely responded with a nod and continued with what he was saying.

When we arrived at his apartment, it was exactly what you would expect of a young creative trying to make it in the big city. It was tiny and dingy. The baseboards were dirty, and layers of paint flaked off onto the floor. There was a small kitchen that also served as the dining room and living space and a bedroom with a caged bird on the floor in the corner. I stooped down by the bird and pretended to be interested in it. I hate birds (they don't have lips, and I don't know how anyone trusts something that can't smile), but chatting up the fowl creature felt like a good way to mask my nerves. Soon, a hipster young woman knocked on the door. I was relieved to have another woman there. The photographer explained that his friend, the woman, had just launched a new clothing line, and we would be shooting her look book.

The designer friend doubled as the hair and makeup artist. She basically applied black eyeliner and then smudged it with Vaseline. She rubbed the remaining Vaseline on her hands into my hair, black greasy eyeliner remnants and all. The shoot went smoothly, other than me having no idea what they meant when they kept telling me to look "strung-out." After a few hours of photos and trying to shield myself while changing clothes in the corner, they sent me on my way. I wandered my way back to the Subway station and rode into the city to catch a couple of casting calls before calling it a day.

A few weeks later, I found myself back in that little birdcage apartment for another shoot. It was the same old drill. As we waited for his designer friend, he chatted me up like an old friend, asking about the jobs I had booked since I shot with him last. He mentioned that he was excited for us to shoot again so he could see how I had grown as a model. He laughed a little and nonchalantly added, "You know, it's so funny that you mentioned that you were a Mormon first thing that morning. Typically, when I shoot with brand-new models, I slip a little something in their drink to help them relax. But I knew a Mormon guy in college, so I know Mormons don't do drugs." I'm sure my face didn't look very modelesque as I tried to stomach what he just said. Weirdly enough, it wasn't just that he said he regularly drugged my peers and almost drugged me that creeped me out. It was how he said it. This guy not only felt comfortable drugging adolescent girls who are essentially alone with him in his apartment, but he also felt comfortable openly talking about it in a joking, lighthearted manner.

I wish I could say I stood up, flipped his crap kitchen table, and stormed out while calling the police to report him. I wish I could say I even told my agency about his brazen brag. Nope. I sat quietly, like a good little model, and did my best to fake a smile as he laughed. I was sixteen and terrified, and I just wanted to do a good job. I wanted to please him and my agency. I knew what he was saying was bad, but I no idea how to handle that situation or the many battles that lay ahead of me as a model. Over the next two years, there would be more promptings that helped me avoid similar encounters, but not always.

I feel deeply blessed for the divine intervention that protected me on this occasion, but in this fallen world, heaven can't always take the bullet for you. Sometimes, no matter how many days you've gone without missing scripture study or how many Honor Bees you have around your neck, bad things do and will happen. It doesn't mean Heavenly Father and Mother are distracted, and it most definitely doesn't mean They are punishing you or love you less. It just means you're a human having a human experience. Francine R. Bennion wisely taught that the knowledge of the gospel of Jesus Christ "makes sense of love and joy and miracles but also of suffering and struggle and lack of miracles." The doctrine of Jesus Christ explains all human suffering, but it does not prevent it. "Nobody is manipulating every human decision that would affect every human experience. If God did, we would have the kind of existence now that Lucifer offered permanently."[1]

Our Heavenly Parents are good parents who allow Their kids to learn and grow through experience. They are not helicopter parents waiting to swoop in at any sign of trouble to shield you. There may be times in your life that it feels like any good Heavenly Parent would have spared you. In fact, it's better that you expect a handful of those moments. Just like a poor petless kid may yell, "When I'm a mom, I'll let my kids have as many dogs as they want!" (Sound familiar, Mom and Dad?), not fully understanding what it means or the work required in or ramifications of having the zillion pets they dream of. We, too, may wish our Heavenly Parents would parent us differently without fully understanding Their motives or wisdom.

Again, our lack of understanding isn't bad. In fact, it is exactly why we came to this earth. We are all new faces here to have experiences that expand our knowledge through the practice of faith and hard work. Faith is striving to believe that Heavenly Father and Mother love you regardless of what you do or don't do because you are part of Them and striving even harder to return the favor.

Note

1. Francine R. Bennion, "A Latter-day Saint Theology of Suffering," in *A Heritage of Faith: Talks Selected from the BYU Women's Conferences*, ed. Mary E. Stovall and Carol Cornwall Madsen (Salt Lake City: Deseret Book, 1988), 53–76.

Chapter 6

Demolition and Remodeling

Change was in the air spring of 2007. I felt a desire to start college in the fall with my peers. I was discouraged that my career hadn't turned out like I had expected it to. I booked shows and enough jobs to get by, but nothing that would ever make me any real money or advance my model career. Funny enough, the fashion industry is much like high school: so much of your success is determined by whether one of the popular kids decides she or he likes you. If a big name books you for their show or shoot, then suddenly everyone wants to sit by you. Success by industry standards always felt just out of my reach. A few times I was put "on hold" for big shows like Prada and Marc Jacobs only to find out my spot had been given to another model the day before. It felt like having the popular girl tell you she was inviting you to her exclusive birthday party and then having your required invitation lost in the mail. Make no mistake about it, I wanted to be a household-name model. I wanted to join my friends at the Met Ball. I wanted the money, the clothes, the attention, and the status I had always dreamed modeling entailed, but I felt stuck. I slowly started to accept that success in this industry was out of my hands. I could have all the right measurements. I could perfect my pout and refine my runway walk, and still never really make it.

As I grew more comfortable taking an honest look at my future as a model and less comfortable with the idea of spending more of my time trying to force the universe to submit to my will, I slowly started remodeling how I envisioned my future.

I went home for the spring and summer to get ready for college and celebrated my eighteenth birthday. Since I can't remember a time since I was eight years old that I didn't have a job, I started working at Costa Vida making $6.25 an hour and getting ready to spend the summer working at a hotel near the Grand Canyon. Much to my surprise, my agents contacted me and asked if I wanted to model for an agency in Tokyo for nine weeks during the late summer and early fall. With the ever-elusive carrot of modeling success dangling in front of my face, I quit my upcoming job in the Grand Canyon and pushed back my first semester of college. The plan was to start college January of 2008 regardless of how the nine weeks in Tokyo went, but I couldn't help but get excited about the possibility of making it big during this trip. Sure, I had struggled to find acceptance to the cool kid modeling table before, but maybe this was my chance! In the life of a model, the possibility of booking the cover of a big magazine or a big show is always just one good casting away. You never know if a big name in the industry will decide to like you tomorrow.

So with one suitcase packed with clothes and another suitcase packed with soup mixes, jars of peanut butter, and Top Ramen, I was off to Tokyo. (Confession: The irony of packing ramen was completely lost on me until less than two years ago.) I immediately loved the city of Tokyo. I was fascinated by the vastness of it. I loved wandering the magical gardens throughout the city with their koi ponds and the Harajuku teenagers dressed like cartoon characters. I lived in a tiny three-bedroom one-bath apartment with two other models, one Polish and one Canadian.

The Polish girl had been in Tokyo for a few months already by the time I arrived. She was so kind to me and spent a lot of time showing me around and visiting sites. We loved people-watching at Shibuya Crossing—rumored to be the busiest intersection in the world—and browsing the trinkets and anime toys on Harajuku Street. This girl was fun and silly, not the brightest, but she was truly kind to me.

Whenever we were on an adventure together, we would always have to make a zillion bathroom stops. The frequent bathroom stops were strange and a little annoying, but I didn't really understand what was going on until our agency started getting mad at our Canadian roommate about her weight.

I need to explain a little about the business of international modeling for this story to make sense. Every model has a mother agency who essentially controls her career and has first dibs on her earnings. My mother agency was Elite. When I worked in another market, Elite would essentially rent me out to another agency in that part of the world. The new agency would work to book me jobs in their area for a contracted period of time. They would take a portion of my earnings, and they would send a portion of my earnings to my mother agency.

The Japanese agencies, in an effort to attract certain models, offered "guaranteed contracts." This means the Japan agency promises the model that she will make a certain amount of money during her stay, and if she didn't, the agency would pay her the difference. It's a pretty sweet deal for anyone who has a few weeks to kill.

The Japanese agency that was interested in working with me offered a guaranteed contract ensuring that, after paying for airfare and lodging, no matter how many jobs I booked in my nine weeks, I would walk away with around $10,000 USD. This was exactly what I needed to start college. A huge miracle.

Because there is so much money on the line, the Japanese agencies are pretty intense about knowing exactly what they're getting. When you sign the contract, you sign next to your bust, waist, and hip measurements. If your measurements fluctuate more than one centimeter, it's grounds for sending you home without paying a dime and often requiring you to refund them for the cost of your flight and other expenses they accrue.

The Canadian girl and I arrived in Tokyo around the same time. They gave us a couple of days for our bodies to normalize after flying before bringing us in to the agency to weigh and measure us. The measuring is done in front of all of the employees and any clients or models currently in the office. There is zero privacy, and it's humiliating even for young skinny models. I was cleared until the next routine measuring, but the other girl was put on immediate probation. They counseled her to eat only rice cakes and to exercise as much as possible. They put her on probation and told her to come back to get measured a few days later.

I felt really bad for her. It was awful to watch how they all acted disgusted and appalled by her measurements. She was visibly hurt as we quietly headed back to the model apartment. That night, she went with some other models to a bar. While at the bar, she met a US serviceman serving on the local base. When she came home the next morning, she was giddy about the handsome, married US solider she had spent the night with.

Over the next couple of weeks, she spent most of her time going out with this man. The nights that she didn't spend with him, they "spent together" over the phone. Our rooms were separated by a traditional Japanese sliding paper wall. During that period, I fell asleep every night to hymns blasting on full volume through my earbuds to drown her out. Now, this girl was a legal adult, and just because her sexual standards and choices were different from mine, that did not give me grounds to judge or slut-shame her, but that doesn't mean little me didn't have a hard time with it all.

Over the next two weeks, she got in more and more trouble with our agency. Staying out late and getting hammered doesn't really help you look fresh for 9 a.m. castings. This is where I figured out why my Polish roomie had to so frequently use the bathroom. One day I walked into the kitchen to find the Polish girl giving the Canadian a handful of pink pills. "What are those?" I asked.

"Oh, my pink pills! They're good for your tummy." She proceeded to explain that a few months ago, she was on a shoot and her stomach felt hard and full. She was bloated. A member of the crew gave her a pink pill to help. A laxative. Now whenever her stomach hurt she would take a laxative. Which, because she was taking them regularly, would make her stomach hurt, which she would treat with more laxatives. I desperately tried to explain to her that she was destroying her insides, but she relied on her pink pills to stay within her required measurements, and she insisted that the crew member who gave her the first one said they weren't bad for her.

Even with the help of a handful of laxatives, our Canadian roommate was sent home a few days later, and we carried on with work. Luckily, I never had a problem with my agency regarding my weight, but that didn't mean I measured up to their standards.

On the same visit into the agency to check my weight and measurement, they gave me a half sheet of paper with a list written in broken English.

Circle all you comfortable model:
- Furs: yes/no
- Cigarette: yes/no
- Alcohol: yes/no
- Lingerie: yes/no
- Sheer: yes/no
- Semi-nude: yes/no
- Nude: yes/no

I quickly circled "yes, no, no, no, no, no, no," handed it back to them, and didn't give it another thought. I was about ten paces out of the front door when the cellphone they just gave me buzzed. They wanted me to return immediately.

All eyes were on me when I walked back into the agency. The owner approached me with the half sheet of paper in her hand and said, "You don't modeled sheer or lingerie?"

"No, I don't." I was pretty comfortable with this conversation, given I had had it so many times over the last two years, but the fact that my mother agency had not told them about my standards made me a little uneasy.

"You miss many jobs and money."

"Oh, I understand. I would rather miss out on a few jobs and keep my standards. It's for religious reasons, and I'm so young."

As her voice got louder, my heart beat harder. "You eighteen! You old enough for lingerie!" she yelled in the best English she could muster through her anger. She followed it with a slew of Japanese in a tone that made me shudder. As she continued to scream at me, I started to realize that this company was planning on me to be their new model to push to lingerie companies. It would kind of be like a football team recruiting a quarterback and then that quarterback showing up saying he only played . . . whatever the opposite of a quarterback would be. A center? Sorry, I'm not a sports kid. Anyway, she was furious. She told me that I would either need to do lingerie or she was sending me on the first flight home and not paying me a dime. She ordered me to go back to the apartment and call with my choice in the morning.

Going home without the money would mean I would have to push back starting school another semester and find some way to make the funds to pay for my tuition and everything else. I was terrified and crushed. I wasn't in a place where I could accept defeat and call quits on the modeling dream. If I returned home early, everyone would know I had failed as a model. I couldn't stomach that.

When I got back to the apartment, I slid my paper door closed behind me, sat on my Japanese mattress on the floor, and bawled my eyes out. Going home would ruin my plans and be completely humiliating. I considered staying and playing by their rules. I would just pretend the pictures never happened. Chances are no one back home would ever know. I could make my money and be done with it in nine weeks. I considered this option for a few moments before deciding that $10,000 wasn't worth everything I had worked for over the last two years. I could hide it from my friends and family, but I knew I couldn't hide it from God. Not that I was worried my Heavenly Parents would love me less, I just knew They expected more from me.

That night, I cried really hard. It was like all of the pressure to maintain my standards within the industry was finally too much for me to handle. I cried and I cried.

The night before my first trip to New York, my Dad gave me a red journal. Inside the front cover, he pasted a print of a painting of the Savior. On the opposite page, he pasted this note:

Dear Rosie,

Way to go America's Next Top Model! Rosie, always remember who got you here and how it came about. You are in the right place doing the right thing. Heavenly Father will continue to direct you as you continue to be worthy of the Holy Ghost.

You can do this. You are a dedicated hard worker. You love adventure and are very mature. You make friends quickly and are a wonderful friend to others. You will be stretched by this amazing opportunity. Enjoy every minute—happy and sad. Don't give up even when you feel like it. Keep a journal. Stay humble. Be professional. Look people in the eye and let them know you are in charge of the product: YOU. Be yourself. Be kind. Smile. Be super aggressive. Help others, but don't let them take advantage of your kind heart. Question and read everything. Learn the business inside and out.

And more importantly hold on to your secret weapon—the Holy Ghost. You can say "NO" anytime, anywhere. People will respect your unusual morals and standards. As you stick up for yourself, you will be surprised how others will stick up for you.

I'm so excited for you. You go, Rosie!

Love,
Dad ☺

As I read these words that I had read countless times around the world, I cried even harder. But this time, I cried because I felt strength. I knew what I needed to do. The decision felt easy, even though I knew the consequences would be extremely difficult. I remember thinking, *This is like what happens in movies. This is the moment when the hero of the story has to make a hard choice and she looks back on it later in her life as the best choice. I have to say no.*

I wrote my agents back home an email explaining what had happened and asked if they could help me get a new contract in another market. Paris, maybe? Then I went to sleep.

I woke up fully expecting to have a plane ticket home by the end of the day. As I got ready to go to the agency, my phone rang. It was my agents from back home. They immediately calmed my fears. They explained that there was nothing in my contract about lingerie, so I wasn't breaking my end of the deal. They had already talked to the Japanese agency and explained that if she sent me home, she would be the one breaking a legal contract, and that she could plan on never getting a model from my agency again. My agents, like the absolute champs they are and as much as my standards were an annoyance to them, stood by me.

In the Japanese business culture, saving face is everything. In order to preserve their relationship with New York, the Japanese agency kept me. But there was a catch. If I booked for a single job that I had to say no to for any reason, they could send me home penniless because I would be harming their business relationship.

And so, the games began. Day in and day out for the next nine weeks, they sent me to lingerie after lingerie casting. They did everything they could to get me booked on a job that I would have to say no to so they could send me home. Luckily for me, and much to the agency's disappointment, the Japanese lingerie clients weren't interested in my boardlike body.

In most markets, the agencies give each model her list of castings and leave her on her own to navigate the public transit system. In Japan, we took the metro every now and then to castings, but most days an agency employee drove us in a van to and from castings all over the vast concrete jungle. It was normal to spend up to eight hours a day sitting in the van. I was usually paired with a group of Russian models who spoke little English, so I mostly sat in silence and tried to get some homework done.

We would typically arrive at a casting an hour before it started (they never wanted to appear late) so there was a lot of sitting. Once the doors opened, all the models would line up. When it was my turn, I'd hand the client my portfolio, they'd then look through it and look me up and down. Sometimes they would ask me to pose, turn around, or walk back and forth. If they had any questions, they would ask the agency employee, and then we'd all load back into the van and drive to the next appointment. It wasn't unusual for the client to point at something in your portfolio or right at you and say something, at which point everyone who spoke Japanese would laugh before waving you away.

It was monotonous and often depressing. I quickly grew to loathe each casting day. I would wake up and think, *Only ten or eleven more hours till I can go back to sleep!*

After about three weeks, I wanted to go home more than anything. I called my parents and explained how much I hated it. They told me that I could come home anytime I wanted, but they encouraged me to stick it out. My sweet parents encouraged me to spend my free time finding things to see and explore. They always reminded me that one day, I would look back on this time and I would never regret adventuring.

I started to make goals for myself that would get me out into the city. I visited shrines, famous towers, and all the standard tourist sites. One of my very favorites was the Tsukiji Fish Market. I woke up early in the morning and took the train out to the warehouse building of roughly nine hundred wholesale dealers. Each wholesale vendor had a small stall made of Styrofoam containers holding creatures I had never seen before—often in their own blood. The workers would grab giant fish from tanks, whack their heads off with massive knives (the fishes' heads), and then skewer them like hotdogs all in one motion. My eyes were going to pop out of my head, but I had to stay alert because workers rushed up and down the narrow isles on motorized carts full of fish and other creatures. When I had enough of the blood and guts, I went to the salmon auction.

The frozen salmon bodies had been stripped of their heads, tails, and fins, but they still looked bigger than me. They lay in rows on the cement floor of a large refrigerated warehouse. Men in rubber rain boots walked up and down the rows and inspected the meat by checking a small chunk cut out of each fish. Their trained eyes looked for specific color and texture to signify the best taste. Buyers representing clients all over the world would bid on and eventually pay thousands for the torpedolike fish.

Shortly, before I left Tokyo, I went to DisneySea, one of Disney's most beautiful theme parks, by myself. I never planned to go by myself. Some of the Russians and I were going to go, but someone always booked a last-minute job and our plans always fell apart. On my last weekend, I knew I would regret not going, even if I had to go alone. The park was beautiful, and the firework show was spectacular. When I asked someone to take a picture of me with Mickey and Minnie, I got stuck posing with them for a crowd of locals that formed. The very best part about the whole day was when it was my turn for the rides. They would ask how many riders, and I would hold up one finger. Confused, they would look around me and see that I really was alone. Then, rather than pairing me up with an odd-numbered group, they would put me on the ride all alone. I want you to imagine sitting in a log on Splash Mountain or a Jeep on Indiana Jones *all by yourself.* I was a little embarrassed and flustered at the time, but it is now one of my favorite memories.

During the week, I would often walk about two miles to the Tokyo Japan Temple. The temple was the one place I felt at home. The sweet temple workers always made me feel like they were excited to see me even though we were never able to communicate. I was always just as excited to see them. When it was my turn for baptisms, the sweet and tiny grandpas would always give my wrist a squeeze when they were done with the prayer and it was time to go under the water. I had to basically dunk myself in weird contortions because the water was so shallow on me. When I was done, I would sit in the lobby and just soak in the familiar spirit before heading back into the concrete jungle. A couple of times I walked through the park across the street, but it was infested with cats and it always freaked me out. On my way home, I would treat myself to a Frosty from Wendy's. I'm convinced that the Frosties in Japan are the best Frosties on earth.

In the summer months, Tokyo has summer festivals what feels like twice a week. Streets would shut down to traffic so locals and visitors could wander between temporary sidewalk stalls. Vendors sold everything from noodles to large beetles in cages. Often my walk home from the temple would be lit up by fireworks from a nearby festival. The first time I returned to the apartment after doing baptisms at the temple, one of my roommates asked, "Where in the world have you been? Did you go swimming?"

As I slid into my room, I said, "Oh. I was at church."

On the other side of my paper wall, I heard, "What kind of church is at 8 p.m. on a weeknight and gets your hair soaking wet?" This is probably why I never made AP on my mission.

Though I wasn't much of a missionary, I loved attending church in Tokyo. The ward didn't really know what to do with me, but a senior missionary couple took me under their wings. Whether this was out of the kindness of their own hearts or by assignment from the bishop, I will always be grateful for the time they allowed me to spend with them and the meals they shared. It breaks my heart that I can't remember their names. I would give anything to thank them for the kindness they showed me.

As difficult as those nine weeks were, they were the beginning of my personal spiritual foundation. During that time, I read and read and read. I read the entire Doctrine and Covenants and a *Teachings of the Prophet* book my mom sent me with.

Slowly but eventually, the majority of my time in Tokyo came and went, leaving me with only a handful of jobs to show for it. Thankfully, none of the jobs required me to say no to a client. Runway castings for Tokyo Fashion Week started about two weeks before my flight home. Runway shows, with their bright lights, hair and makeup, and elaborate costumes, reminded me of dance performances. Though I always felt nervous right before a show, I was always filled with a surge of immense confidence once I had both stilettos on the runway. After a slow seven weeks, I was thrilled to book a few shows.

When you book a show, you have to go a few days ahead of the show for a fitting. At the fitting, the designer puts you in a few outfits, called "looks," to decide what they want you to wear in the show and determine where you will fit in the lineup. I was thrilled to book the Junko Koshino show because she was one of the biggest designers in Tokyo—and because she looked exactly like Edna Mode from *The Incredibles*. At the Junko Koshino fitting, one of the very first outfits they put me in had a sheer tank top. The tank top didn't bother me, but the sheerness was pretty extreme. I carefully asked the woman assigned to help me get dressed if I could wear a bra. "Bra? Bra?" as I motioned to cover my chest. Confused, the dresser shook her head and repeated, "No bra. No bra."

I walked out of the fitting crushed. Again, for a moment I considered just saying yes. It would have been so easy. Just one show. One shot at the end of the runway was all I would have to hide from. As easy as it would have been to accept this fate, I knew I had to say no, and I knew they were going to send me home empty-handed. I mentally accepted that the whole summer sitting in a van was wasted. Heartbroken but at peace, I called one of the agency employees whom I had built a little friendship with and told her about the tank top. She told me to hang tight and that she would see what she could do. I don't know what she said to them, but she quickly called me back and explained that I needed to go to the mall and buy a stick-on bra. Somehow, without any type of incident, she had convinced them to let me wear a bra under the sheer tank top.

In my journal, I complained that the stick-on bra cost me 8,000 yen (roughly $70 USD) and then finished with, "Oh well. It's a small price for my dignity." Oh, the drama.

With music blaring and noise from the crowd finding their seats, the other models and I quickly dressed in our first looks. We all had metallic nails and black bluntly cut bob wigs. As the dressers organized us in the proper order, it was clear a few of the models noticed that my look was a little different from theirs. One sweet girl said, "I wish I could be wearing a bra. I hate having my picture taken wearing this sheer stuff." It breaks my heart to think of how many young girls in that industry do things that they don't feel comfortable doing simply because they don't know they can say no. It breaks my heart even more to know that there are young girls all around the world in schools, work places, and even families who still need to master this skill.

I'm so grateful that my dad made sure that I understood how to say no. Saying no is a skill we can all benefit from. Saying no to things that make you uncomfortable takes courage, but it is so worth it. Even in the Church, we can improve at and feel more comfortable saying no. We are often taught, especially as women, to always say yes within Church culture. Say yes to feeding the missionaries, say yes to the callings, say yes to watching the neighbor's kids, say yes to making the ward member a meal, say yes to giving a talk this week.

Brené Brown, hallowed be her name, says:

> One of the most shocking findings of my work was the idea that the most compassionate people I have interviewed over the last thirteen years were also the absolutely most boundaried. . . . Boundary is simply what's okay and what's not okay. What I think we do is we don't set boundaries. We let people do things that are not okay or get away with behaviors that are not okay, and then we're just resentful and hateful. Me? I'd rather be loving and generous and very straightforward with what's okay and what's not okay.[1]

Should we serve and sacrifice and give? Yes! Should we serve and sacrifice and give ourselves into the ground? No!

> And see that all these things are done in wisdom and order; for it is not requisite that a [woman] should run faster than [she] has strength. And again, it is expedient that [she] should be diligent, that thereby [she] might win the prize; therefore, all things must be done in order. (Mosiah 4:27)

Learning a healthy balance between saying yes and saying no within the Church is hard. There will probably be some judgy whispers, and you may even be tempted to judge yourself. Exaltation is not won by whoever gave away the most casseroles. Regardless of how many times you say yes, you will still be saved on the condition of receiving the grace of Jesus Christ. We are saved by Him, not the number of used cans of cream of chicken soup. You are better able to serve if you care for yourself. Sometimes you need to stretch and say yes even when it is difficult. Sometimes you need to say no even when it is difficult. Together, you and heaven can figure out when those times are. If anyone in your ward gives you side-eye for passing on the sign-up sheet, give yourself a healthy boundaried high-five and just shake it off.

I think one of the lessons we all are tasked to learn in this life is the balance between works and grace. I've heard a lot of people try to explain how to have both in your life, but the best explanation I have ever heard is from Samuel M. Brown in his book *First Principles and Ordinances*. He says:

> An analogy from my professional life may clarify the needed balance between faith and works. My primary research and a significant amount of my clinical practice focuses on how the body regulates blood pressure. In most people, as long as the average pressure stays in a generally acceptable range, the blood pressure takes care of itself through some complex and fascinating physiological mechanisms. There are two examples of extreme ways blood pressure regulation can fail: shock and malignant hypertension. In shock, the body is no longer able to maintain a sufficiently high pressure, and the body's organs fail quickly. For shock, we infuse adrenaline and saline solution into the veins in a desperate attempt to raise the blood pressure. On the other end of the spectrum, there are patients whose blood pressure rises so high that they are no longer able to regulate it down. We call this condition hypertensive emergency or malignant hypertension. To fix this problem, we administer medications to block adrenaline and dilate blood vessels as well as diuretics to remove fluid from the body. These conditions, shock and malignant hypertension, represent opposite extremes in the regulation of blood pressure. Their treatments are antithetical to each other. As I've pondered the relative roles of grace and works in repentance, I have come to see those two ends of a spectrum, as treatments for spiritual imbalances. In my analogy grace raises blood pressure, while works lower it.
>
> We tend to like things to be the same for every person. "Don't talk too much about grace or there will be no room for works," on the one hand, and, "stop all this talk about works; we need grace," on the other hand. But without context these conversations are confused and potentially dangerous. Just as

dilating blood vessels in a patient in shock is dangerous, so is talk of grace a terrible idea for a person who currently needs just enough courage to behave righteously. On the other hand, giving adrenaline to a patient with malignant hypertension is as bad an idea as preaching works to a drug addict who needs more than anything to be able to imagine that someone, somewhere could love him. For some of us, the right answer will be an emphasis on grace, while for others the right answer will be a strong emphasis on the need to measure up through works.[2]

In the last few years, I've recognized that I have developed the habit of always telling myself that I need to improve in the works department while rarely allowing myself to benefit from grace. If I'm always pushing myself to do more, accept more responsibilities at church, work, home, or in my community, I can tell myself that I'm working hard. No one can argue otherwise. But someone could make a strong case for the fact that I'm acting as if my salvation is dependent on my abilities. If I sacrifice enough, then I will be saved. In truth, Christ has already paid the price. Yes, I have a responsibility to do my best, but I will always be saved by grace.

———— ———— ————

The Junko Koshino show went smoothly. The only problem was a portion of the runway led down floating stairs to a lower level. Men seated under the stairs would look up our skirts as we went up and down. So besides having grown men looking up the skirts of children, my Edna Mode wig and stick-on bra made me feel like a boss. I later found out that Junko decided to use the picture of me at the end of the runway as a massive banner image in her flagship store, stick-on bra and all. Japan has strict nudity laws, so having a shot of a model from the show without her bare chest showing turned out to be of great use to them.

After the show, we all crammed back into the small dressing area and began the process of changing back into our normal clothes and returning our wigs. Members of the Junko Koshino team filled sparkling flouts with champagne and distributed them to the models. All the other girls looked glamorous as heck. Meanwhile, I was in the corner trying to peel my bra off—which is anything but glamourous—but I was just happy that it all worked out so smoothly.

Shortly thereafter, my Tokyo time was up. The day before my flight home, I stopped by the agency to give them my apartment keys and collect my money. The agency employees glared at me the entire time they counted out the money they owed me. I felt a little bad collecting so much money when I had only booked a few jobs, but then I remembered how much time they wasted by sending me to lingerie castings in the hope that they could send me home. After that, I didn't feel so bad anymore. With the paperwork signed, I said my tearful (JOKING) goodbyes and took the stack of yen to a money changer in Roppongi Hills near my apartment. With my fresh wad of USD, I was ready to go home.

The next morning, I got up, tidied up my little room for the next model, and headed out the door. I needed to take a cab to the bus stop that would take me to the airport. Only then did I realize that even though I had enough credit leftover on my bus card to cover the bus fare, I didn't have any physical yen to pay the cab driver. I didn't have enough time to go back to the money changer, and I knew the agency sure as heck wouldn't help me, so I began to drag my two massive suitcases up and down the steep Tokyo hills to the shuttle. About halfway into the journey, the wheels on one of the suitcases busted off. So soon I was pushing one suitcase in front of me and dragging the other one, wheel-less, behind me. I was sweating like an animal and feeling pretty sure I wouldn't make it. I tried to make eye contact with cab drivers as they drove and hoped one would take pity on me. Some hills I would have to push one suitcase to the top and the run back down to the bottom for the other. When I think about eighteen-year-old, 105-pound me trying to get 100 pounds of luggage to that bus stop, I have to laugh. I wish you could have seen it.

With a few thousand dollars in cash wrapped in paper and duct taped to my gut for safe keeping, I made it home. I didn't know for sure if I would ever go back to modeling. Still not satisfied with the outcome, there was a part of me that wanted to try again. But the other part of me, exhausted by the constant battle, knew it was time to hang up my stilettos and call it quits.

One of the most frustrating parts about my modeling career, for me and my agents, was always feeling like there was so much potential, but that I couldn't reach it without cutting the moral code that kept me grounded. Surely, many girls have healthy and moral careers in this industry. But for me, due to the level and style my look lent itself to, I couldn't have both. Looking back, I can see that there are lots of contributing forces to why my career didn't boom the way we all had hoped. Maybe I just didn't have the right look. I surely didn't have the passion and desire to sacrifice everything for it. As much fun as a huge career would have been, I'm grateful that teenager me felt comfortable saying no to anything that made me uncomfortable.

I'm grateful for this, not because I think a racy photo or two would ruin me, or that I couldn't be a good Mormon without a perfect photo record. I feel grateful because I, from a very early age, knew that I had value that was worth respecting. I could say no to anything without need for explanation. If I or you don't want to do something, for any reason, we always have the right to say no. Will there be consequences? Sure. I never really made it in the fashion industry because I said no and I said it often, which meant it ultimately wasn't profitable for my agency or for me to continue. That and I didn't have the exact look the industry was looking for at the moment. At the time, I felt like a failure, but these days, it feels like a lucky break. You will never regret standing up for yourself, no matter how painful the consequences are to swallow. Who knows? Maybe you'll be grateful for the consequences down the road, like I am.

I think this is where Christ really shines. His ability to take bummer situations and turn them into something of value is truly impressive. He gave sight to a blind man with mud made of dirt and spit. He healed a man by instructing him to wash in dirty water. And He developed my Spirit by allowing me to be a "close but no cigar" model.

Notes

1. Brené Brown in The Work of the People, "Brené Brown on empathy, compassion and boundaries . . ." Facebook video, March 5, 2016, https://www.facebook.com/theworkofthepeople/videos/10153967066765682.
2. Samuel M. Brown, *First Principles and Ordinances: The Fourth Article of Faith in Light of the Temple* (Provo, Utah: Maxwell Institute, 2014), 48.

Chapter 7

A "Has-Been" at 18

To this day, there are still people who seem disappointed when I tell them I am no longer pursing modeling. They are usually women, and my guess is it's because they imagine modeling to be the most glamorous and exciting thing someone could do. With a fair amount of time, prayer, and therapy (always therapy), I have learned that I can and have a responsibility to do bigger things in this life than walk well in a straight line in high heels.

That being said, I don't look at fashion magazines, and I don't follow my friends who are still in the industry on Instagram. Why? I think there will always be a part of me that is drawn to the idea of that lifestyle. In modeling, you can make a lot of money really fast. I had a seventeen-year-old roommate who, in 2006, was making $25,000 every day she was on set. Call me crazy, but that will always be appealing. When I see my former roommates on the red carpet with celebs or shooting on magical islands, I start to wish I could trade my little home with green carpet and wood paneling for that life. I have a great life, and I love my little home. I don't like feeling ungrateful for the blessings I have been given so I choose to focus on what I have and not on what I don't.

After getting denied by BYU, I started my first of what would be three semesters at Dixie State College January 2008. Dixie was one of the best things that ever happened to me. At Dixie, I made the kind of friends I had dreamed of and we played nonstop. We went boating, to the dunes, to Vegas, hiking, swimming, four-wheeling, and off-roading. While at Dixie, I got involved with the Student Ambassador program. This program offered scholarships to students who helped with high school recruiting. Within this program, I developed a lasting confidence and speaking skills that have blessed my life immensely. I loved visiting the high schools and inviting potential students to learn more about this place that had introduced me to so much happiness.

One of the happiest things about Dixie was they were always giving away free food. I *love* free food! And the best kind of free food is free corndogs. One sunny day, I was walking down the center of campus eating a free corndog and felt a level of happiness that I hadn't felt since I was a tiny kid. I was completely satisfied with what I was doing and where I was. After I called my mom and shared the good news that a semi-cold corndog had solved all my problems, I started what would be years of studying happiness.

What had changed? Why was I suddenly so much happier eating a corndog in St. George, Utah, than I ever was looking at my face in a glossy magazine in New York?

Somewhere between studying geology and biology curled up in an armchair by the big glass wall at the back of the old Dixie State library and eating quesadillas at 2 a.m. with my roommates, I discovered that I had a powerful mind. When I used that mind to learn new things, I did really well in school. I got the same thrill from acing a test as I did from walking a runway. The only thing that was different was that the feeling of satisfaction and accomplishment I got from using my mind lasted so much longer.

I played hard while at Dixie, but I worked harder. When I wasn't studying for exams, I was working as a receptionist at a local gymnastics studio and in the ambassador office on campus. At the end of my three semesters, I was finally admitted to BYU.

When I was applying for colleges in the first place, I applied to BYU because that's where everyone in my family went, and Dixie was my one backup because that's where a friend from high school was going. When I didn't get into BYU, I was crushed. Getting denied by any college hurts, but getting denied by the college your church owns has a special sting to it. I was totally embarrassed, annoyed, and discouraged. However, it turned out to be the biggest blessing. Going to Dixie was an important stage in my development—and I didn't have to take American Heritage. In fact, because I got a 4.0 while at Dixie, I was able to transfer to BYU and get a full tuition scholarship. I felt like I had truly swindled the system, and I told just about anyone I could about it. Clearly, I'm still over the moon about it.

Another important stage to my development was my Mormon mission in the faraway magical land of Mesa, Arizona. Sweaty Dansko clogs and long skirts were a far cry from stilettos and skinny jeans, but I was okay with that. Just like every good Mormon missionary, I fell in love with the people of my mission—which was so easy to do considering the fascinating and unique culture. (That's my very best missionary version of a dad joke.) But in all seriousness, nothing feels better than getting a glimpse of what God sees in someone, especially when that person is tricky to love. On my mission, I learned that the best way to love someone is to serve them. Service is Heavenly Mother and Father's love language. Their love language is especially cool because whether you are giving or receiving this love, it makes you happy.

Chapter 8

Likes DO NOT Equal Love

When I signed my modeling contract, I thought I had found the answer to all my problems. Not only was I trading math class for Milan, but I was, finally, going to be seen. Regardless of my faithful parents' efforts to raise me to understand my divine nature, I was convinced that my worth was tied to my appearance and the world's acceptance of it. People told me I was living every girl's dream and, for a moment, I believed it. I believed that as I found my face in bigger and bigger magazines, I would be happier and happier. It is no secret that the world teaches that one of the greatest things a woman can do is to be seen and praised for her appearance. Much to my dismay, confusion, and downright annoyance, being seen and praised for my appearance didn't change anything.

Though I physically left the industry shortly after I turned eighteen, my mind circled back to my modeling career for many years. What was that all about? Was I getting Punk'd? What happened to my *New Era* cover dreams? Why was "every girl's dream" such a bummer? Was I broken or simply the most ungrateful daughter of God? Why didn't I feel any happier?

As I began my study of happiness, I realized that when I was in middle and high school and when I was a model, I basically only thought about what I looked like to other people. You know that feeling when you're at a party and so nervous about what people think of your outfit even though everyone is probably too concerned about their own appearance to notice yours? No? Just me? Well that was my life from about twelve to eighteen years old. I was basically constantly having an out-of-body experience as I obsessed over what I looked like to the outside world. Sure, this makes me sound insane and weird and shallow as heck, but when you consider the constant onslaught of messaging focused on women's appearance, can you really blame me?

I, like so many women, was obsessed with self-objectification. Though I could tell you I was a valued daughter of Heavenly Parents, deep down, I saw myself as an object for other people to look at. Studies show that when women's brains are focused on their appearance, they struggle with academics like math and reading comprehension and perform worse at athletics.

In today's world, women don't need to be on the glossy pages of *Vogue* for validation because they have Instagram.

"My last 'gram got so many Likes that I now feel ultimate and true love and acceptance," said no woman ever. Likes do not equal love. No matter how many followers you recruit or how much engagement you log, it will never fill your love cup. But again, can we really blame ourselves for trying?

Let's be real. We all know someone, maybe she's a babe Laurel who looks like she's twenty-five or the babe mom of four who looks like she is twenty-five who posts endless selfies or sexy body shots with cheesy anonymous motivational quotes in the captions. Nothing pairs better with cleavage and Kylie Jenner duck lips than "Dance like nobody is watching." I know, I know. It is *so* easy to get level-10 judgy when we scroll into these 'grams. But before you screenshot it and send it to your friend with an eye-roll emoji, consider that maybe, just maybe, that's the only way she knows how to feel acceptance. Has the little Kylie Jenner Jr. in your life ever been praised for her brain, wit, work ethic, skills, or abilities? Or has she been hypnotized by "You're so pretty" and "I wish I had your body" her entire life?

Remember that before we came to this earth, we were in a place of ultimate love and acceptance, and our poor little spirits simply miss it. Let's do our best to ease the homesick spirits around us by giving compliments that matter more. I bet you can remember a time when you felt the Spirit (a heavenly compliment) after completing a hard task or goal or after serving someone. But when was the last time you felt the Spirit burning in your bosom because your curls were the perfect beachy status? I'll wait.

At the end of this life, would you rather hear "Well done, my good and faithful servant" or "You look pretty"? Let's compliment like Christ.

Chapter 9

The Temple Is Important, but It's Not Because of the Tulips

Have you ever had one of those mornings where you wake up sans shrill alarm and just feel ultimate comfy? Your room is both the perfect level of brightness and temperature, and your bed feels like the comfiest place in the whole world? When we die, I hope we get to take a one-hundred-year nap in those conditions before anything else. Okay, so obviously I have zero idea what it will be like after we die, but the following is what I tell myself it will be like . . . post-celestial nap.

I wake up in a dark tunnel with a bright light seeping in from the end. (I know, I know, *so* creative, right?) Anyway, as I make my way down the tunnel toward the light I hear cheering. As I get closer, I begin to decipher what they're chanting. Over and over they chant *my* freaking name! Instinctively, I pick up my pace to a light but athletic and motivated jog. Think: Nike commercial of a woman jogging on a misty tree-lined road. Scratch that. Think: Beyoncé, jogging. The cheering gets louder and louder. I can see myself bursting through the barrier of light at the end of the tunnel.

Through adjusting eyes, I make out a giant stadium full of people. I squint to recognize individual faces in the crowd. I see family members, friends, coworkers, and neighbors. My heart will surely skip a beat when I see the faces of some Jewish and Muslim kids I made friends with while studying in Jerusalem. There will be some faces that I don't immediately recognize, but I like to think that something in me will know they're moms that I helped seal to their children or women I helped make covenants in the temple. I'm excited to see faces of people I wouldn't expect to see. People who I wrongly judged or misread, yet people who are loved by God and receive His grace. It will be a happy and humbling experience.

Simply because I'm a strong believer in giving the people what they want (within healthy boundaries), I'll make a lap around the stadium with my hands reached out for round-the-house high-fives. Naturally those out of high-five range will be doing the wave. Once we've attended to that important duty, I'll run down a tunnel of especially loved ones, high-fiving me and smacking my butt all along the way (with my enthusiastic consent). At the end, I hope I'll find my Heavenly Mother, Heavenly Father, my Big Brother Jesus and my big sis Eve. I get chills thinking about that group hug. It's just gotta feel something like getting a massage and having your hair played with while holding a baby—scratch that: holding a puppy, while watching a perfect sunset with shooting stars, on a mountain, at the beach, in pajamas, while eating Arby's with Taylor Swift.

Just as a girl who has been away for summer camp excitedly tells her parents about everything from the giant spider she found in the tent to perfect afternoon at the lake as soon as she gets home, I'm going to want to tell them about everything I did while on this earth. Okay, so yes, they'll already know everything I did, but I'm telling them anyway, and you can't stop me. I'm going to tell them about that one time when I was nine that I rented a party pony and rode it around the backyard for an hour on a random summer afternoon. I'll ask them if there is any way I could rewatch that one time my childhood dog Archie jumped into the back of the Suburban when the back door was still closed. Preferably they would have this scene recorded on slow-mo and looped. I want to tell them about how much fun I had making friends and adventuring with four refugee teens. I'm also going to tell them about all the skills I gained while I was away. I learned how to do statistics (kinda), how to make really good tacos, how to build a company, how to teach a dog to do trust falls, how to cross-stitch Taylor Swift lyrics, and a few more things that I hope they'll be able to use in the kingdom. Side note: after all of this, I want to spend ten years talking to all of my dogs—Sunny, Pete, Max, Reuben, Martin, Dale, Archie, Willie, Ted, and all of my future pups—and thank them for being such good boys. However, I have zero desire to see our family pet bird, Copper, because he was a monster.

Now, I know our Heavenly Parents will be kind and excited about just about anything I return and report on, but wouldn't it be semi-awkward if my report went something like: Jesus, thank you for all that you did that enabled me to go to earth. You'll be proud to know that while on earth I was a total babe and had tons of followers on Instagram.

All the crickets who lived nice cricket lives and made it to heaven will surely be chirping.

I know I'm not dropping any new truth bombs when I start talking about the weird messaging from the media that teaches women and men that the ultimate accomplishment for women is to reach ultimate babe status. But have you ever considered how we might be teaching this within the Church?

Next up? "Your body is a temple."

I would like to meet a young woman raised in the LDS Church who hasn't heard this phrase. We might as well have it tattooed on our backs, but of course we all know you wouldn't graffiti a temple, right? Often, "your body is a temple" lessons focus on the temple's appearance, the beautiful grounds and clean walls. The common correlation is that young girls should also be beautiful and clean like the temple. Sometimes when something is repeated a zillion times, the true meaning of the teaching gets lost or obscured. Let's talk about "your body is a temple" a little bit and see if we can get back to the meat of it.

I want you to imagine two missionaries in the home of an investigator. Scratch that. Two missionaries, teaching an investigator, in a member's home. Everyone knows the Spirit is stronger when there is fake ivy and vinyl letters on the walls. The two sisters have been preparing all week for this important lesson. Tonight, they're teaching their investigator, Miriem, about the temple, and they've fasted and prayed that she will really feel the importance of what they teach her. As the smell of brownies wafts through the air, they open with a prayer and begin the lesson with a prop, because these aren't like normal missionaries—these are cool missionaries. As they hold a picture of the Salt Lake Temple between them, the senior companion leads out:

"Miriem, this is just one of the many temples that spot the globe. Temples are some of the most important buildings on earth because (dramatic pause) look at these tulips." Junior companion builds up the courage to add, "Temples are sacred because look at that reflecting pond!"

What's wrong with this picture? Not the actual temple picture . . . though I think many of those are way too Photoshopped to look like glowy castles. We're talking the big picture! Are temples important because they are pretty? Maybe to the random visitor, but to anyone who has a knowledge of the restored gospel, the answer is NO. Temples matter because *inside* of them we take part in soul-saving ordinances that enable us to fulfill our purpose and return to God. Temples are important because they help us connect to heaven. They help us learn how to become like Christ. They are a place for peace and reflection. They give us opportunities to serve others.

Our bodies are like temples because they, too, house something sacred. Our bodies are the current home of spirit daughters and sons of God. Our bodies are important because of what they hold and what they do. Our bodies are not important because they are beautiful for others to look at. Sorry, not sorry. They're just not. Our bodies are tools that help us in the process of becoming like Christ. They enable us to serve others. They help us feel the Spirit and feel closer to our Heavenly family.

If the beauty of temples is not the most important factor, why does the Church dump buckets of money into maintaining elaborately landscaped grounds or Egyptian marble stairs? Again, because of what happens on the inside. The beautiful temple exteriors only pay homage and respect to the sanctity of ordinances within. Like temples, out of respect for what is on inside our bodies, we should treat the outside of our bodies with care. We should do our best to keep them healthy and well groomed, but we should beware of measuring our value based on our exteriors or any teaching that focuses more on our outward appearances than on our hearts. At the end of the day, even if a graffiti mob ravaged the once-pristine temple walls, or if the skies rained down straight acid mud and permanently marred the exterior, the temple would be no less valuable. Outside forces cannot touch, harm, or alter the virtue of the temple. The same goes for you.

Before we end this lesson, I would like to draw one more parallel. The temple is the house of God. God has the ability and right to decide who enters His home. Your body is your spirit's home. No one has the right to touch or interact with your body without your consent. No one.

When I was in second grade, I was invited to the cool girl in the class's birthday party. Her name was Michelle. Michelle had long wavy brown hair and barrel-curl bangs that would make any '90s girl swoon. I, a scrappy kid with a bowl cut, thought she was incredibly beautiful. Simply out of respect for this seven-year-old queen, I stressed over the perfect gift to bring as my offering. After much thought, I decided a Caboodle was really the only gift fit for Michelle. I remember carefully wrapping the pink and purple tackle box while fantasizing about what life with my new BFF Michelle would be like. The day of the party arrived, and I couldn't wait for my new future with Michelle as besties to begin. After we ate cake and ice cream, we all sat in a circle around Michelle as she opened the gifts. When my turn was finally up, I carefully handed her the perfectly prepared Caboodle. Michelle quickly tore the wrapping, glanced at the Caboodle, weakly gave a "thaaaanks" without making eye contact, and then passed it to her mom so she could devour the next present. Like Roxanne to Max in *A Goofy Movie*, "she looked right though me." My little heart was shattered. Maybe she didn't see the tissue paper I wrapped and taped around the handles to protect them.

Jesus Christ died, in part, so you could have your body. Our bodies are unique gifts, perfectly designed and fit for each one of us. They're Caboodles. When we disrespect, trash talk, or misuse our Caboodles, that's gotta make Him feel a little like baby Rosie getting shut down by baby Michelle. The good thing is, He is a good dude and gets it. He gets how tricky it can be to appreciate a Caboodle when homegirl next door has a Lisa Frank art kit. But at the end of the day, He gave us Caboodles because He loves us and knows what we need. Take a timeout from the comparison circus and look inside your Caboodle. Discover the specially designed compartments and start filling them with cool stuff.

Our Heavenly Dream Team—Heavenly Mother, Father, and Brother—for sure wants us to respect and care for our bodies, but I think They'll be more excited to hear about what you did with your mind and heart, how you filled your Caboodle, than how many Likes your OOTD got on Instagram. But honestly, they're such sweeties, I'm sure they'll be happy you're happy about your suede booties too.

Our big sis Eve is a pretty good example of a woman who bit the bullet and decided to do more with her Caboodle. Eve made the very the brave choice to leave her cushy life in the Garden of Eden and face life in the world so we could all come to Earth, get bodies, and learn stuff. Jesus, like any ideal big sibling, lived His life in a way that would serve as the perfect example for all of His little siblings. He also suffered and died so we can all one day leave this place of learning and go back home with bodies and knowledge intact.

I still have lots of spiritual work to do before I can begin to understand what Jesus and Eve have made possible for us. Not to mention the generations who came before us who enable us to live the specific lives we live. My grandmas spent hours and hours training in fine arts. They then raised their children to appreciate the arts. Those children became my parents, who made sure I was artistically literate, which has served to be an absolute pillar in my life. My creativity feeds my soul, offers comfort when I'm overwhelmed or confused, and pays my mortgage. Creativity is in our spiritual DNA because it is what we are.

As Elizabeth Gilbert said: "I myself am a product and a consequence of Creation."[1]

We are blessed to walk paths cleared by our trailblazing predecessors. Just think of all the medical and technological advances that we take for granted every day. I lived before the time of iPhones, and to prove it, I have a story about hitching a ride home from a dark park on a winter night when I was fourteen because my dad forgot to pick me up while he was at the ward Christmas party. We are all blessed by the women and men who fought for equal rights in the Civil Rights Movement. As a single woman, with an education, who votes, owns her own home, and runs her own business, I feel a profound sense of gratitude for the women who have sacrificed and fought for my rights for decades.

We have been given much. And much is expected. When you really think about all the hard work logged by endless people that enables you to live your life, it's hard not to feel a sense of responsibility. As we travel paths cleared by those before us, we have both the privilege and responsibility to do big things. Many of the people who fought for the privileges we enjoy never got to experience them in their own lives. We owe it to them to capitalize on their work and follow their lead by blazing new trails. The trail blazers, with weeds up to their ears, don't often get to enjoy the path they clear, but we owe it to the generations before us and the generations after us to blaze on regardless.

In this, like all things, Jesus is the raddest example. When Jesus healed the blind man on the Sabbath, He was, by the established Jewish church and cultural standards, breaking the rules. He knew the current popular trail was off course. Correcting it meant pushing into the weeds on His own. Jesus encouraged those around Him to follow His example by acknowledging our limited understanding while seeking to improve and learn more, with faith and modern revelation. He encourages us to do the same today.

Yes, we came to this earth to get bodies. I don't know about you, but I got my body twenty-nine and counting years ago. If I came to this earth just to get a body, why am I stuck here suffering through bad dates, street harassment, The Black Eyed Peas, and food that expires before I get to it? If this was all just about getting bodies, I am pretty sure Heavenly Mother and Father and Their Only Begotten Son, the most creative trio *ever*, could have come up with a more efficient plan. The truth is, we aren't just here to get bodies. I resist putting words in Christ's mouth by defining His motives, but I think we can say, thanks to the help of scripture and modern revelations, Christ came to this earth to get a body. However, He also came so He could gain experience. Alma 7:13 teaches us that the Spirit knows everything and could have taught Christ anything He needed to know about how to be a good Savior, but Christ chose to come and learn for Himself through personal experience. And because of those experiences, He knows "how to succor his people" (Alma 7:12). So when I have experiences that I just don't know how to deal with, it helps to know that Christ knows how to deal.

A while ago, I was swiping into my sorrows on Bumble. I came across a handsome dude—we will call him Homeboy—and noticed we had a bunch of mutual friends. I liked most of our mutual friends, so I swiped right and we matched! I made my dutiful first move and sent him a witty message that was probably written by my copywriter friend, Maggie. He responded, but then I started going on some dates with a Tinder match, so I never got back to him. A few weeks later, when the Tinder match burned out, I redownloaded Bumble. Much like trying to figure out if you have anything edible while standing in front of a pretty bare fridge, I casually surveyed my existing matches. I came across Homeboy and sent him a little note apologizing for never getting back to him. It probably wasn't my best work, so I don't blame him for not responding, but at this point I really wanted him to. A few days later, I texted one of our mutual friends and asked if he was a good dude. She responded that she didn't know him well, but what she did know about him she liked. She suggested I just reach out to him on Facebook rather than depending on the temperamental algorithm of Bumble. Maybe he deleted Bumble? Sliding into the DMs of this dude felt bold, and I wasn't sure if I felt like I could own it. But I did. I DM'd him this:

> Homeboy, We matched on Bumble and keep missing each other. I feel like we have a better chance on FB because rarely does it make me so flustered that I delete it. Your ex-match and pending Facebook friend, Rosie

On July 20 at 8:12 a.m., Homeboy read my DM, and on July 20 at 8:12 a.m., Homeboy didn't respond. On July 20 at 8:13 a.m., I felt like the Mayor of Rejectedville, USA. I was sure Homeboy was screenshotting my DM and sending it to people who knew me. I could see them texting their LOLOLOLOLs while sitting perfectly quiet.

Obviously, in the grand scheme of world peace and hardship, my DM drama is NBD. But it is in these small personal moments I like knowing that I have a Savior who once had a member of His closest crew reject Him. I'm not saying this was a hardship that I needed the Savior to carry me through, one footprint in the sand style. What I am saying is whether I'm laughing off a cringy dating experience or stomaching an actual trial, I'm glad I have a Savior who can say, "Yeah. I've been there," or who has the wisdom to know that sometimes the most comforting thing is "Yeah, that sucks." (Your Jesus may not say "sucks," but mine does.)

Like Christ, these kinds of experiences are what we came to this earth for. When I left home at sixteen and started working around the world, Michelle Reedy, a family friend, said to me, "There are two types of education. One you gain from formal schooling like college. One you gain for life experiences and travel. Both are important." We came to this earth to gain both book smarts and street smarts because both are important parts of becoming more like our Heavenly Parents. Our earthly experience has been designed our Heavenly Dream Team to help us as we progress in this life and the next. IDK how my ability to cross stitch "Haters Gunna Hate" is going to help build the kingdom, but I'll leave that up to those at a higher spiritual pay grade to figure out. But let it be known, that if the need for funny cross stitching in heaven arises, this girl is ready to answer the call.

Note

1. Elizabeth Gilbert, *Big Magic: Creative Living Beyond Fear* (New York: Riverhead Books, 2015), 96.

Chapter 10

To Be Learned Is Good

When I was in Young Women, if you would have asked me what my purpose was, I would have likely said something about becoming a good mom. I knew education was important, but mainly because I wanted to be able to care for my family if something happened to my husband. Whenever a girl friend said something about not going to college, I was quick to encourage her to go because "What if something happened to your husband?!" Education was strictly a Plan B financial safety net.

Wrong, wrong, wrong!

Eva Witesman gave a flawless BYU devotional on this very topic called "Women and Education: 'A Future Only God Could See for You.'" Woman or man, *you need to listen to this talk*. If I could, I would cut-copy-paste the whole thing right here.

I feel like this bit explains it beautifully:

> In a world that values education primarily as a means to increase our value in the workplace, nonlinear educational paths may sometimes be considered nontraditional, but they are *not* nonessential. As Kristen Oaks observed, "Women's educational paths and experiences are often very different from men's." As Latter-day Saints, we know that the pursuit of education is not merely about gaining marketable skills in an efficient and linear fashion but that education is a tool for gaining important spiritual growth and spiritual gifts that can be used in all facets of our lives.

Okay, but this one too:

Our intellectual and spiritual growth through education is a righteous pursuit and represents our willingness to fulfill a commandment of God. Investments in our own development are worthwhile because we are daughters of God, and He wants us to reach our divine potential in every possible way. But it should also be acknowledged that it is virtually impossible for the influence of a Spirit-led education to end with only our own benefit.[2]

Last one, I swear:

Sisters, never question the value of your education or wonder whether you will have an opportunity to learn and use the knowledge you have gained. God knows you, and even though you may not yet know His plans, He knows the end from the beginning. He is preparing and qualifying you for the work He wants you to do. He will continually guide you to ways in which your knowledge and skills can be of benefit to yourself, your family, your community, and His kingdom.[3]

The purpose of every child of God is to develop Christlike attributes as we, like Christ, grow and become the person God sees in each of us. We each have a work to complete on this Earth. A path to blaze. A battle to fight. Just as the Savior was the only one who could complete the task He was called to complete, we, too, each have a responsibility to a mission unique to each of us.

Our Heavenly Dream Team is very creative, and They know us very well. They have numerous tools they can use to help us along our paths. Regardless of what life experiences or tools they choose to use in your life, the purpose is to help you learn and grow. No tool is better than another. There is no right or wrong way to become like Christ. There is only the way you and the Heavenly Dream Team work it out together.

Ok, now those of you that think I'm dissing the calling of a mother can calm down. I'm not diminishing motherhood/maternity in any shape or form. Motherhood is one of those things that we've talked about so much that we may be a little fuzzy on the specifics. Motherhood, actual having and caring for children, is a tool that our Heavenly Parents use to help many many women become who they are supposed to become. It is a high and holy calling that is vital to the plan of salvation. The Heavenly Dream Team needs women and men to team up in the process of bearing and rearing little humans so more spirits can come, learn, and return home more like Christ. Parenthood is a sacred opportunity to practice being like our Heavenly Parents. I'm guessing this isn't new info to any of you given it is foundational to our doctrine. We do a really good job teaching this in the Church. It's a major focus, and for good reason.

Do you know what else is a high and holy calling? Whatever your Heavenly Parents call you to do. As I write this, I'm twenty-nine years old (I think I have said this three times by now, but I just feel like adults don't get enough opportunities to tell people how old they are). I'm single and don't have any human children . . . that I know of. (JOKING) I do have a dog named Ted (#theodorecard), who is pretty much too pure and good for this world. We really don't deserve him and his pup paws. Is my life purpose as a woman on hold? Am I stuck in the pregame waiting for main event to start? Heck no. Our Heavenly Parents, or all people, understand that life is short. In no way would They waste a single day. If you are single and feel like you are in a holding pattern until your E.C. and co. come along, snap the freak out of it! Ain't nobody got time for that! You need to start taking your life and your purpose seriously.

Yes, I would love to have children of my own. The highs and the lows—I want it all. But that isn't the life I have been given. (At least not yet!) So what am I supposed to do with the maternal instincts I have aching inside of me? I use them! I smother Ted with so much love it makes people around me uncomfortable. (Note: If dog moms make you uncomfortable, sorry, not sorry.) I use maternal instincts to love and serve a family of teens from Rwanda. I use my maternal instincts to manage and grow my business. Does acting within your motherhood when you're sans children take creativity? Yes. Does it take hard work? Yes. Does it take patience? Yes. Does it take problem solving? Yes. Can it be discouraging and heartbreaking? Yes. I could keep going, but the point I'm trying to make is I am learning all the same principles my sisters and friends with children are learning. We are just learning from different textbooks.

Regardless of what textbook you're learning from or what lesson plan Heaven has written your name at the top of, we all have a responsibility to learn. We have a responsibility to study things out, weigh our options, make choices, and act. Heaven sent us here to progress, not just survive an allotted amount of time.

Just like a hesitant little sister may look to an experienced big sister as an example, we can look to Eve. Eve was sent to this earth to complete a very important mission. She came to this earth with the power and authority to turn the key that initiated the plan of salvation. Her calling came with huge responsibility and a healthy dose of ambiguity, but Eve did not shrink. She did not shirk her responsibility to her husband or wait for someone else's approval. Though we don't know all the details yet, I like to think that Eve studied her choice to eat the fruit out in her mind. She weighed her options and their consequences, and then she made a choice. She was brave in a way that I can only dream of being. Rather than being surprised by her bravery, maybe the better response would to see her bravery as a confirmation of her divine nature as a woman. "Women are surely beloved of the Lord for Him to have placed them in such a position. As He relies on women to embrace the greatest law, to bow to the greater commandment, He affirms their intellect, their integrity, and their righteousness."4

Sheri Dew said, "I believe that the moment we learn to unleash the full influence of converted, covenant-keeping women, the kingdom of God will change overnight."5

Luckily, Adam was smart and good man. Though initially unsure of her choice and cautious to follow, he listened to his wife's wisdom and joined her in their mission (#couplegoals). Though we may not be accustomed to the idea of a wife leading out in large choices in a marriage, if the first couple is to be our first example, then maybe we should be. Leading out sometimes means taking the first step alone. Being a leader feels risky and often lonely, but if you have a true partner, you won't have to feel that way for long. Beverly Campbell put it beautifully when she wrote, "Their thoughts and actions are to be united and purposeful. Their strength is to be found in their oneness and in their identifying themselves to all others as a whole unit."6

Shortly after I graduated from BYU, I moved to Salt Lake and started working in the video department of the Church. I worked hard and saved my money. In the fall of 2014, we had a particularly grueling shoot schedule. For about eight weeks, I was flying between shoots in

Guatemala, New York, France, New York (again), Utah, and Jackson Hole. I think I was home a total of seven days during that time. By the end of this period, my body was shot. After all of the travel, long days, jetlagged nights, and eating out, I felt like a soggy slug. I remember thinking, *I wish I was married because then I would have a nice blender wedding gift and I could make super healthy green smoothies every day to help my body heal.* I don't know what slapped me across the face, but I like to think it was the Spirit, because something slammed me in that moment. What the freak was I waiting for? I called my mom, and with the help of her Costco card, I went to buy my own freaking nice blender. No wedding registry needed. In that moment, I started my life.

Seventeen-year-old Rosie was sure twenty-one-year-old Rosie would be married. Twenty-one-year-old Rosie was determined twenty-five-year-old Rosie would be married with two kids. Twenty-five-year-old Rosie was too busy working hard with the tools her Heavenly Parents picked for her to use in her process of becoming to think about what twenty-eight-year-old Rosie would be doing. It turns out that twenty-nine-year-old Rosie (four times) is just really excited and grateful and way too busy to spend too much time trying to guess what any future Rosie will be doing.

If you're reading this and thinking anything along the lines of "But motherhood, with actual human children, is the most important thing a woman can do," please consider that Eve was known as "the mother of all living" well before baby Cain and Abel made their grand entries. The truth is, everyone loses when playing the comparison game. Not all women are called to bear and nurture children on this earth. It is a really sad and painful truth. Yes, we have been taught that everyone will have the chance to be a parent in the next life, but the most important thing for a woman to do in this life is whatever her Heavenly Parents call her to do.

For you, right now, it may be caring for your offspring. For me, so far, it is building a company that helps women feel more comfortable in the house of the Lord and writing a book. For your neighbor, it will be something completely different. Rather than focusing on the differences in our details, why not focus on what we all have in common? We are all doing our best to become like Christ using the tools we have been given. Putting one tool above the other doesn't make using your tools any easier and it sure as heck doesn't help you make new friends. And we all could always use more friends because between misleading Tinder photos and toddlers, life just isn't always easy.

In this light, I think it is easier to see how girls can (read: should) be starting off their journey as women around the same time that young men begin their journey as priesthood holders. For young men, holding offices in the Priesthood is one of the tools, like fatherhood, our Heavenly Parents have designed to help boys become like Them. There is a structure they follow to help them track their progress. They get started on their journey at twelve, and so should we.

Believe it or not, Personal Progress was not designed to drive Young Women leaders insane or to keep girls busy while the boys are working on their Eagle. Personal Progress is a tool to help structure and track the personal progress of girls in becoming like Christ. Think of any skill you think it would be cool to have. Now consider this: how could Personal Progress help you actually *progress* toward that goal? Wild, right?! How would our young women be different if Personal Progress was used to help learn new skills and gain knowledge rather than a necklace (that will likely be a tangled mess in a box or lost all together in within three years)? How rad would it be if young women were given examples about working well with coworkers and spouses in lessons on patience? "Very rad!" yells the reader.

I'll tell you one way our young women would be different. They would be happier. Here is why.

As women, we are hard wired to be creators. Our actual bodies are designed to make little humans. That is wild and sci-fi and *cool*! But, given all that we talked about above, we could stand to expand our definition of our divine mandate to create. The responsibility to create doesn't kick in when the baby starts kicking. If you're old enough to be reading this, you're old enough to be creating, ring on your finger or not. Now easy, cowgirl. I'm not sanctioning teen pregnancy or premarital sex (however, if you do get pregnant before marriage, God and we love you and your baby—obviously). When I bought my own blender, I did more than give my days a healthier start. When I bought my own blender, I gave myself permission to dive headfirst into my purpose as a woman (a.k.a. creator, teacher, leader, protector, and more things that end in -er/-or) and it was one of the most liberating, most powerful, happiest choices of my life. It was like my eyes were opened, and for the first time, I could see that I had zero time to waste. Heaven had sent me here on a mission. And for some wise purpose, I am meant to serve the first part, and possibly the whole part, without a companion. I mentally got up, got dressed, and went to work. It took faith, and it has been hard (like raising a kid must be), but it was a step I wish I would have taken a decade sooner.

When we create something that wasn't there before, there is something inside of us that says, "Ooh, that felt good," because it's what we came here to do. One of my favorite things to ask moms is if they ever have moments when they look at their little humans and think, *Holy crap, I made that.* Whether they physically grew their children inside of them or not, most moms' eyes light up at this question because all moms make and mold little humans into big humans, and that feels rad. Exhausting, annoying, harrowing, and stretching, but rad and exhilarating too.

How do I know that feels rad? Because even though the tags are still attached to my baby maker, I'm creating in a manner designed by my Heavenly Parents every day. Sometimes I create in little ways, like making muffins in doughnut tins. Sometimes I create in big ways, like building a company. Sometimes I create in important ways, like helping a Rwandan refugee experience what it is like to be a kid in America. No matter how you create, it will feel better than any compliment on your appearance ever will. (Except if that compliment is from another woman about your eyeliner, because those compliments make me feel like the queen of the world.)

In the words of Sheri Dew:

> While *we* tend to equate motherhood solely with maternity, in the Lord's language, the word *mother* has layers of meaning. Of all the words they could have chosen to define her role and her essence, both God the Fathe and Adam called Eve "the mother of all living"—and they did so *before* she ever bore a child. Like Eve, our motherhood began before we were born. Just as worthy men were foreordained to hold the priesthood in mortality, righteous women were endowed premortally with the privilege of motherhood. Motherhood is more than bearing children, though

it is certainly that. It is the essence of who we are as women. It defines our very identity, our divine stature and nature, and the unique traits our Father gave us.[7]

All women are creators, and all women are mothers. As a childless woman to women with children, please don't judge me or think less of me because I mother differently than you. Motherhood is a lot of things, but it most definitely isn't a competition. Motherhood is truly a high and holy calling no matter what unique way God has designed for you to mother. The only thing that may feel as good as getting a compliment on your eyeliner may be having another woman see and support your unique efforts to mother.

If you're like me, childless and chill, it's time to move beyond any notion that you're in a waiting period or holding pattern phase. You and your mission are too important for that. Get to work. Start creating. You will learn the lessons about life and yourself that will only bless you in the future, no matter what the future looks like. Sure, there will still be lonely nights, awkward questions about your dating life at family parties, and sometimes even heavy hearts during Sunday school lessons on "The Family: A Proclamation to the World." That's life. The good news is you will find happiness and satisfaction you didn't know was possible.

Notes

1. Eva Witesman, "Women and Education: 'A Future Only God Could See for You'" (Brigham Young University devotional, June 27, 2017), 4, speeches.byu.edu.
2. Witesman, "Women and Education," 5.
3. Witesman, 6.
4. Beverly Campbell, *Eve and the Choice Made in Eden* (Salt Lake City: Deseret Book, 2002), 42.
5. Sheri L. Dew, *Women and the Priesthood: What One Mormon Woman Believes* (Salt Lake City: Deseret Book, 2013), 163.
6. Campbell, *Eve and the Choice Made in Eden*, 57.
7. Sheri L. Dew, "Are We Not All Mothers?" *Ensign*, November 2001.

Chapter 11

Queen of Light

On my mission, (ah, the familiar start to every mission story that feels important and interesting to only the person sharing it) we sometimes met our investigators for lessons at Mesa Temple Visitor Center. We loved VC lessons because we could sit in comfy chairs in well-air-conditioned rooms and watch movies. One of the movies we loved to watch was about the life of President Monson. There is this really sweetie part when President Monson says, "I always want the Lord to know that if He needs an errand run, Tom Monson will run that errand for Him."[1] President Monson did an incredible job at acting fast on promptings, and little Sister Card was really moved by his example. Ever since then, I have tried—very imperfectly—to live life similarly. I want my Heavenly Parents to know that if there is an errand that needs to be run, They can count on their girl Rosie.

Mid-January of 2015, I was in the temple praying about my job situation. For the last year, I had been working at the Church in the video department. I worked full time, but I was technically a contracted employee. My boss, Jim Dalrymple, was assigned to support and record the Big 15's (The Twelve and First Presidency) international travel and teaching. Jim hired me consistently to his projects and was extremely generous in what he taught me. My time working for the Church had been amazing. I had traveled the world and literally sat at the feet of Apostles and listened to them teach. But at this time, policies were changing, and I felt like my job at the Church would be changing soon too. As I sat in the temple, I was having a heart-to-heart with heaven, and my mind was wandering like it does every time I pray. Was I supposed to start looking for a job at another company? Could I get enough freelance photo and video work to financially support myself? I thought about an entrepreneurship (a word I have never spelled right the first time) class I took at BYU. I loved that course, and ever since then, I had wanted to start my own business. I thought of all the boss young women I "knew" via social media who ran little clothing shops of their own. I loved the idea of running a company like them, but I wanted to solve a problem. I wanted to fulfill a need, and they were already doing a rad job at providing inexpensive and cute clothes to the Mormon world. I loved that they had some many cute dress options for sale. *You know what I wish they had?* I thought. *Cute temple dresses.*

Pause.

Someone needs to make cute and comfy temple dresses. And then I felt the Spirit nudge me and say, "Why don't *you* make cute and comfy temple dresses?"

Pause.

"Okay! Fine. I will!"

I'm going to make cute and comfy temple dresses. At that moment, a mental gun shot off in my mind, and I started *booking* it! I'm not sure I heard a single word of the temple ceremony I was participating in from that moment on. As soon as I was done in the temple, I got dressed, went upstairs, and scheduled an appointment for early the next morning with Sister Samuelson, the Salt Lake Temple matriarch. On the drive home that evening, I wracked my brain and made a list of every single person I knew that had some connection to the manufacturing world. I made a quick stop at Walmart to pick up some food because a girl's got to eat. While shopping, I called my parents and told them the good news. I had figured out what I was meant to do: I was going to design a temple dress line! I'm not sure how much they actually thought it would happen, but bless their souls for being as just as excited about my new little creation in the making as they are each time one of my sisters announces she is pregnant.

Less than two hours after receiving the idea, I was emailing friends, family, and acquaintances who I could possibly glean any wisdom from. I even emailed people and asked who they knew who could help me. Asking for referrals in faith, just like I practiced on my mission.

Before I finally crashed in bed, I googled, "how to start a clothing company," and opened the first five or so results so they'd be ready for me in the morning. The next morning, dark and early, I was pitching my idea to start a new kind of temple dress company to Sister Samuelson. I ended my rough and underdeveloped presentation with, "So, am I allowed to do this?"

As I write this, I think I'm just appreciating for the very first time how important her response was. She could have said, "That sounds like maybe something you should have more experience in" or "I think the temple dress options we have are fine." In that moment, she could have let her own opinions or fears extinguish my little flame with the pinch of her fingers. But she didn't. Sister Samuelson, blessed be her name, whether she realized it or not, offered me an armful of kindling. "I think you should go for it. It's about time." Together, we reviewed the temple's requirements for temple dresses, and then I was quickly on my way. As I was gathering my things, President Samuelson walked by. Sister Samuelson signaled him in and said, "This is Rosemary Card. She is starting a temple dress company!" and with that, she sealed the deal.

That idea that eventually grew into a full-blown company. Q.NOOR has been a tool that has taught me and changed me in ways I can't explain. My well of compassion for customer service personnel runs deep. It's been three years since I met with Sister Samuelson, and Q.NOOR still kicks my butt on the regular. I was inexperienced and unqualified for this job. Bless Sister Samuelson for encouraging me to have the faith to blaze new trails rather than discouraging me by suggesting I take the "safer," more traveled road. My life and the lives of many others have been blessed because of it.

Sometime within that first week, I decided that I needed to determine how I would define "progress" and "success" in this new venture. I was extremely hopeful that this new venture would be a means of supporting myself and my pup, but I knew enough about small businesses to not bank on that right away. I took an honest look at my savings and decided that if I was careful, I could afford to invest $5,000 into this project. I then had a real heart-to-heart with my Heavenly Parents. I would put $5,000 and one year of solid hard work into this idea. And even if at the end of 2015 and my $5,000 I still didn't have much to show for it, I would count the process and experience as a win. An expensive and time-consuming win, but a win nonetheless. I think I was really blessed in that moment to be more focused on what I could learn from the experience rather than what I could earn. What this company could do for others felt more important than what it could do for me.

I also decided I need to give this little baby company a name. I'm a sentimental monster, so I knew the name need to hold deep significance for me. I knew I didn't want the word "white" in it. For three reasons. One: most of my would-be competitors have the word "white" in their name, and I didn't want to get confused with them. Two: I didn't want to always be constricted to "white" products as the company grew and expanded. Three: The name needed to be unique for search engine optimization purposes. With some time and a lot of thought, I came to the idea of Q.NOOR.

While studying abroad in the Middle East a few years prior, I learned about the former queen of the Hashemite Kingdom of Jordan, Queen Noor. Queen Noor—a young American who married the Jordanian King Hussein, who was both shorter and significantly older than her—is a fascinating woman. She is known throughout her country and the entire world for being kind and good. She celebrates and champions women in and outside of the home. Her focus on humanitarianism has shaped and blessed the country of Jordan for decades. I adore her and admire the legacy she tirelessly builds. When I first learned about her, I decided I wanted to name my first daughter Noor. "Noor" is the "Jane" of the Middle East. Since I don't have a daughter, I decided to name my company "Noor."

The really magical thing about the name is the meaning. *Noor* is the Arabic word for "light." Arabic is the closest language to Aramaic, which is what Christ spoke when He was on this earth. The *Q* in Q.NOOR stands for "queen." Though I have been deeply inspired by Queen Noor, the "queen" in Q.NOOR is actually not in reference to her highness. When my sisters and I were little girls, my mom taught us that the temple was where mommies went to learn how to be queens. When I visited the temple for the first time, my heart was touched when I came to understand how true that little childlike teaching was. Though I would later get a fair amount of pushback from people who didn't like the name, something about "Queen of Light," Q.NOOR, has always felt just right.

Over the next few months, I spent the vast majority of my spare time after work, and sometimes *at* work (whoops) researching. Initially, I was fairly quiet about this new project, but soon I grew too excited about its potential to keep it to myself. I know lots of people keep new business ideas on the DL out of fear someone will steal it from them, but I liked having people who would keep me accountable. If my friends at work knew I was working on a new company, they would be following up with me, which means I better have some progress to report on.

Ever since I was little, I have been obsessed with horses, cowgirls, and rodeos. During my photography business years, I was the Kamas Bull Wars photographer. I would stand up on the rails of the bucking shoots right next to the bull riders and capture all of the action. At the end of the night, I would be speckled in mud and manure and insanely happy. There was something about creating those pictures that fueled my soul. One of my favorite images from the Bull Wars is the back of a bull rider. Bull riders wear thick reinforced vests that protect them from getting gored by a bull's horns. The fancier vests are embroidered and detailed, but most of them are dirty and black with stickers slapped on the back. This particular cowboy had a sticker on his back that read, "Say I won't."

Not everyone I told about Q.NOOR was as supportive as Sister Samuelson. I was starting a business I had no business starting and that scared a lot people. When we catch even a whiff of failure, the natural reaction is to protect the person in danger by shielding them and sending them in the opposite direction. It is so easy to project our own fears on others and subconsciously attempt to derail them in the process. Luckily for me, my decision was already made and their doubts only fueled my fire. Each time someone responded to my excitement from a place of fear, my little spirit smirked and said, "Say I won't."

Now, when it comes to business ideas, you should always be open and listen to trusted sources' advice. Some ideas really are bad and likely doomed for failure. Like my idea for a small device that parents can snap onto their toddler's shirt if they have a pool. If the device is submerged in water it will trigger an alarm to go off in the home. I still think it's a genius idea that someone should make zillions of dollars off, *if* they can get around the whole electrocution issue.

Listening to trusted sources could save you a lot of pain. Obviously, this applies to more than just business ideas. Most of my trusted sources voiced concern that with such a niche market I would have a really hard time being profitable. I totally agreed, but my success wasn't defined by being profitable. I sure as heck hoped it would be, but that's not what it was about. Success was in the act of acting on a prompting I had received and learning from the process. I also had a gut feeling, one I couldn't describe, that this was going to work.

So yes, listen to trusted outside voices, but at the end of the day, your life is between you and God. You are the one who will need to answer for promptings received and live with the consequences. Both good and bad. People who love you want to protect you. Their desire to protect you usually has roots in their own personal fears of failure. Discouraging a venture that they may be too scared to take feels good to them. Then they can carry on with their lives and forget about it. But you are the one who will have to live with the "what if."

> "Of all sad words of tongue or pen, the saddest are these: 'It might have been.'"
>
> —John Greenleaf Whittier[2]

In this life, it is so easy to be crippled by fear of the unknown. "I don't know" has been the death of so much progression. Truthfully, I am so grateful I didn't know what I was in for. If I could have seen all of the work, road blocks, tears, pain, scary emails (mad Mormon moms are the stuff nightmares are made of), and struggle coming down the chute, I'm sure I would have said, "Actually, thanks for the idea, heaven. Super sweet of you to think of me, but a nine-to-five job sounds super like the best fit for me." I didn't let the fact that I knew next to nothing about manufacturing stop me from acting. Heavenly Mother and Father fully understood my ignorance, and yet They gave me the idea anyway. Crazy, right? It's almost like a parent encouraging a child to walk. Does the parent know the child can't walk? Obviously! They also know the child is going to fall a bunch, but they know it will be the best step for them in the long run. When all the fearful voices, both interior and exterior, said, "Don't risk it," I focused on where the idea initially came from.

> Did I not speak peace to your mind concerning the matter? What greater witness can you have than from God? (D&C 6:23)

"I knew it, and I knew that God knew it, and I could not deny it" (Joseph Smith—History 1:25). I was acting on a prompting and doing my best to "come what may, and love it."[3] Plus, if it did fail in terms of profitability, at least I tried. There are worse things than failure.

"To become queens and priestesses we must be business women."

—Eliza R. Snow[4]

Shortly before launching Q.NOOR, I suffered from a serious case of cold feet. I was moments away from calling it quits when I decided to go to Barnes and Noble for some inspiration. By heaven's grace, I picked up *Big Magic* by Elizabeth Gilbert. I want to cry when I read the notes of encouragement and dreams I had for Q.NOOR in the margins. Next to this quote there is a little heart:

> The rewards had to come from the joy of puzzling out the work itself, and from the private awareness I held that I had chosen a devotional path and I was being true to it.[5]

If we truly believe we are sent to this earth to learn, which at this point I hope you do, then should we really be surprised when God asks us to do things we don't know how to do? Are we really that thrown when we read about God asking Nephi, a kid from the landlocked city of Jerusalem to build a boat? Of course he doesn't know how to build a boat, and of course I didn't know how to create a company. It's kinda the whole point. How are we supposed to grow if God never asks us to stretch? We can't let what we don't know hold us back.

I know stepping into the dark is scary, and let's be honest, it's risky. But let's have a little faith in our Heavenly Parents. Luckily for us, They've done this a time or two. They know how to help Their children get home with pockets full of experiences and knowledge. Will we return home with banged up shins and scratched up arms?

Totally. The Savior has a few scars from His earthly journey too. And because of His scars, ours will be spiritually healed. I know that when we talk about the Resurrection, we traditionally talk about how we will be perfect and unblemished, but part of me hopes I can keep some of my battle scars. To me, they stand for a fight well fought. The Savior kept His scars because they represent His work and His purpose. So can ours. Though I may always sustain wounds from various times in my life, over the years I have come to see them as battle scars and appreciate them as symbolic reminders of vital lessons already learned.

After eleven months of sample development, website building, paperwork, phone calls, emails, checks, flights, photoshoots, and research, I launched Q.NOOR on November 20, 2015. By that evening, I was both exhausted and relieved. With just weeks and very little of my initial $5,000 to spare, I reached my definition of success. Whatever happened from that point on was up to the Heavenly Dream Team. Because of this outlook, I honestly wasn't that overwhelmed or flustered that day. Yes, it was stressful, and I was really hopeful people would buy dresses, but I felt a fair amount of peace because I knew I had done my best. Which was uber convenient because I got dumped that night. The guy I had been dating for the last three months called me and said, "The costs of dating you outweigh the gains. You're just not a worthwhile investment for me." Just let that one soak in for a bit. It's my favorite dating story now because it really was the worst/ most perfectly timed and worded dump ever, but it was pretty much the last thing I needed to hear that day. Before you think this dude is a total monster, in his defense, much of our short relationship was long distance, and he has a very logical business mind. He didn't mean to be cruel. He felt like he was just being practical. After some time passed, we were able to talk it out and I explained that he probably should never say anything like that to another human again. He remains a valued consultant and friend.

When I launched Q.NOOR, there were five styles on the site. With a clean white modern design, QNOOR.com looked like a legit company's site. Other than a few spelling errors, you would have never known I built the site myself and shot 99 percent of the photography in my parents' garage.

While working in the fashion industry, it was so obvious that they have a problem with lack of diversity. Runway show after runway show was a lineup of European-looking white girls, a token black girl or two, and maybe sometimes an Asian girl. When it came time to find models for Q.NOOR, I felt a responsibility, and still do, to do my tiny part in representing more women than just white women. I spent hours on Facebook searching friends of friends for girls who didn't look like your standard white Mormon from Draper. Not that there is anything wrong with being a white, blonde Mormon . . . says the white, blonde-ish Mormon. Finding an ethnically diverse lineup in Utah was harder than I expected, but the time I've spent finding diverse models is time well spent. Women of color are well worth the work. They, like everyone else, deserve representation.

Sometimes I wish I could know what those first models thought when they showed up to the first Q.NOOR shoot in my parents' garage. The morning of the shoot, my dad helped me set up the dove-gray seamless paper backdrop I rented from a local camera shop. I steamed the dresses on the rack I bought the night before at Walmart with my visiting teachee's steamer. I couldn't afford to have a professional hair and makeup artist, so I asked the models to come camera ready. I did my best to embrace the bootstrapping startup appeal, but I was so nervous and embarrassed that I had to force myself to make eye contact with the models as they arrived. In my heart, I knew Q.NOOR was going to be big and legit one day. I knew we would have real photoshoots in studios with photographers, hair and makeup, and assistants. I knew this was just a step toward that future, but I felt anxious that the people around me may not believe I would ever get there.

The five dresses that the models wore in the shoot were the only five Q.NOOR dresses that actually existed. When manufacturing your own clothing, factories require you order minimums of a few hundred at a time. To start production on those five styles, I needed upward of $30,000, and I nearly cleaned out my savings getting to that point. I went through the process of making a pitch deck and talking to investors, but bringing in outside money never felt quiet right—nor did anyone make me any real offers. I decided to do my own version of an unofficial Kickstarter campaign.

When someone placed an order, they knew they were buying a dress that didn't exist—yet. All orders were on a presale basis. I explained to customers that I was preselling a dress to raise the funds to start production. When production would start and when I could deliver a finished product was determined by how quickly I sold enough preorders. By early January 2016, I was about eight weeks in and I'd sold roughly fifty dresses. I wanted to kiss every one of the women behind those fifty orders, but fifty wasn't anything near the few hundred I needed. This is where I had another real talk with heaven. I had been sitting on some of these women's money for nearly eight weeks, and at that rate, I wouldn't be delivering dresses till the end of that year. Either something had to change or I needed to refund the money, close the site, and hide in a hole for a while. The most frustrating part was knowing in my gut that there would be women interested in Q.NOOR. I was just having the hardest time finding them. Even then, as embarrassing and disappointing as waving my white flag and calling it quits would be, I knew I had done my best. Yes, that would be a deep wound to sustain, but I knew I would survive.

Late December 2015, Morgan Jones, a writer for the *Deseret News* reached out to me. Morgan found out about Q.NOOR and my story because we were in the same ward. Though we knew of each other, we still would have left a seat between us in Relief Society. Luckily, a mutual friend, Matthew Ray Banks, told Morgan that if she was in need of a story, she should give me a call. When she did call, we talked for about an hour, but she was sure to tell me that she didn't know if the story would be approved. Though I had high hopes for an article, I had learned years before that you haven't booked a runway show till you have both stilettos on the runway.

On January 11, 2016, Heavenly Father and Mother performed a miracle. The featured story on the homepage of Deseretnews.com read: "Former New York model launches LDS temple dress company," by Morgan Jones.

And then the Red Sea parted. In the article, Morgan shared my story and the beginnings of the Q.NOOR journey more eloquently than I ever could, and the thing spread like wild fire. Emails poured in from as far as New Zealand requesting interviews. Media sources from all over the world started picking up my story. Seeing my little company featured on the DailyMail.com, random towns' news sites, and Reddit was wild. For weeks, people were sending me links to new websites sharing my story. One night, my mom called me to tell me that the *New York Times* had picked it up. I did a happy dance in my bed as a read the piece in their "Women of the World" section. The piece ended with a quote from the original *Deseret News* story:

> "The goal is not to sell a trillion dresses, . . . even though that would be fantastic," Card said. "The purpose of this is to help me become who Heavenly Father wants me to become, so I'm working on that, and it's great that I can try to help others in the process. I know that between Heavenly Father and I, that's the goal."[6]

My little journalist heart had always dreamed that I would one day be in the hallowed pages of the *New York Times*, but never in my wildest dreams did I imagine that my testimony would be.

During this period, I felt a special connection to the brother of Jared. I'm sure he worked pretty hard gathering and preparing those stones he asked the Lord to touch, but at the end of the day, they were just a pile of rocks and he knew it. Only heaven knows how hard I worked to make Q.NOOR, but even after thousands of dollars, months of work, and a couple of buckets of tears, it was a very scrappy little hodgepodge company. The website copy had spelling errors, the lighting in some of the photos wasn't the best, and the dresses for sale on the site literally didn't exist. It was pretty much a pile of rocks and I knew it. But with the touch of the Lord's finger, those rocks turned into lights. Trust me when I say I was just as surprised as the brother of Jared to see the Lord's hand and His work. Many days in a row ended with me crying big happy tears of gratitude because as the *Deseret News* story spread around the globe, the orders started pouring in.

Within just a couple of weeks after the *Deseret News*'s story, I was able to start production on the first few styles. The remaining styles started shortly thereafter. I bought Matthew Ray Banks a very nice present for his wedding a couple of years later.

"Do your best and He makes up the rest." This is a common phrase we hear in Sunday school or YW lessons, but I think it comes up short. The Atonement of Jesus Christ isn't a gap filler. He doesn't swing around when you've checked of all of your boxes and give you a trophy for trying. Christ is with us every step of the process. I worked my freaking butt off to build Q.NOOR and still do to this day. Building, launching, operating, and growing this company has been a full-blown fistfight since day one. Yes, there have been shocking record-breaking sales days and victories, but there have been just as many embarrassing failures and disappointments. This has been anything but a smooth road, but I have never felt prouder of anything in my entire life. Even though I know how much work I put in to this company, I know the driving force that motivated me the entire way was the enabling power of the Atonement of Jesus Christ. While I am the sole CEO and founder, I always know that I have a business partner in Him.

Q.NOOR is two, soon to be three, years old. The brand has gone from being a random idea to a fast-growing company online and with a brick-and-mortar store in Salt Lake City. As I look back on the past four years, I'm overwhelmed by how much I have learned and, in turn, how much I didn't know when I started. There are little things like figuring out how to source clothing labels and branded shipping supplies. Then there are big things like structuring marketing campaigns that utilize multiple platforms and the legal process of transitioning from an LLC to an S corporation with shares. Just like it boggles my mind to think that my earthly parents let me move to Singapore all by myself (Hi, Celine!) at sixteen, it boggles my mind that my Heavenly Parents prodded me to start a clothing line on my own with next to zero manufacturing or business experience. Well, in truth, I've been hustling people for money since I was old enough to break rocks on the sidewalk and sell them to other kids as local crystals. But besides that, I was pretty clueless. Praise the heavens that I stayed ignorant to my ignorance until I was in too deep to turn back. Praise the heavens for seeing both Q.NOOR's and my own potential. Through all the success and growth, there has been stretching, discomfort, and disappointment.

I have faced problems that felt too complicated and risks that felt too scary for me to navigate on my own. But luckily, I haven't always had to. Yes, The Heavenly Dream Team has always been there, but for the most part, I have felt their help through others. For the first six months I folded, packaged, and shipped every single order out of my parents' home. My mom and little sister spent a lot of late nights helping me fulfill hundreds of orders. You don't know loathing folding until you've needed to fold two-hundred full-length dresses in less than twenty-four hours. Sam Wright and Timmy G. Hansen, both extremely successful business men, have proven to be invaluable consultants to bounce ideas off and brainstorm with and are always willing to lend a listening ear. Mike Glauser helped edit the website copy. Nearly every guy I have dated in the last three years has played an important role as a consultant, hype girl, marketing advisor, or business mentor. Karlie Brand Guymon has advised me and encouraged me through the whole process. Maggie Franz has written many Q.NOOR Instagram captions and website copy. She and Kristine "Teen" Metcalf have held my hand through the design process of several Q.NOOR products—not to mention being significant contributors to my "Q.NOOR brick and mortar" Pinterest board. Teen especially has spent hours sending screenshots of design inspiration back and forth. Lee Hale is always there to hype me up when I need someone to help me reach higher. My uncle Rick Evans has helped me through every legal decision and action since day one. Friends and family have been my models, makeup artists, photographers, bookkeepers, and florists. And all this doesn't even mention the thousands of friends on social media who have tagged their friends on Q.NOOR posts, sent in photos to share on Q.NOOR social media outlets, or even just sent encouraging DMs. The more I think about it, the longer this list gets. Long story short, there have been countless people who have helped Q.NOOR become what it is today. It takes a village!

I hope you are able to step back from the names of strangers here and see the community of people who have helped build Q.NOOR in nearly every aspect, from the foundation to the spires. Yes, I spend a lot of days working alone, but I always know I have a laundry list of experienced and successful humans who have proven willing to support me and Q.NOOR in whatever way they can.

Why is this important to you? Good question. I think it can serve as a good reminder to surround yourself with good people. If you're rubbing shoulders with people who are hustlin' hard, you are likely to do the same. You will also be blessed to be able to learn from their examples and wisdom. If you surround yourself with entitled people who lack motivation, you, too, will probably have a hard time kicking yourself into the higher gear that is necessary to accomplish big things.

Notes

1. Thomas S. Monson, *On the Lord's Errand* (DVD, 2008).
2. John Greenleaf Whittier, "Maud Muller" (Boston: Fields, Osgood, and Co., 1870), 15.
3. See Joseph B. Wirthlin, "Come What May, and Love It," *Ensign*, November 2008.
4. Eliza R. Snow in "An Elevation So High above the Ordinary," *At the Pulpit*, accessed March 20, 2018, https://www.churchhistorianspress.org/at-the-pulpit/part-1/14-an-elevation-so-high-above-the-ordinary-eliza-r-snow.
5. Elizabeth Gilbert, *Big Magic: Creative Living Beyond Fear* (New York: Riverhead Books, 2015), 113.
6. Morgan Jones, "Former New York Model Launches LDS Temple Dress Company," *Deseret News*, January 11, 2016, https://www.deseretnews.com/article/865645269/Former-New-York-model-launches-LDS-temple-dress-company.html.

Chapter 12

Follow the Tapping

Back when I first arrived in the mission field, I had two companions. One, my designated trainer, who I bothered because I wasn't who she expected me to be. I, trying my best to be brave, acted without her encouragement, and that made her uncomfortable. My other companion felt like my designated caregiver. She was quick to laugh at the insane missionary moments throughout the day. She made me toast in the morning and wrote me sweet notes of encouragement that carried me through the painful, blistering-hot Arizona days.

My very first area was in the heart of Mesa and bordered the Mesa Arizona Temple grounds. If you could see a snapshot of every street contract in that area, there would be an old truck in some stage of restoration and a yard of spray-painted green rocks in each one. I arrived in Mesa in late July. On my very first morning, my companions and I left the member's home where we all shared a bedroom to walk the track of Mesa High School a few blocks away. It was 6:30 a.m. and blazing hot. As I stepped outside, I noted the similarity between the moment and every time I had stood in front of an open oven. I also thought, *I cannot do this for eighteen months.*

On a main artery road that ran down the middle of the area, there was a small row of government subsidized apartments that we often visited only during the day. Mission folklore shared whispers of missionaries who were once innocently caught in the crosshairs of a violent crime at the complex after dark. When I first got wind of this story, I asked my trainer for a complete retelling of said violent crime. I was part curious, part scared for my safety, and part desperate for even a wisp of something exciting. She shook her head and declined to speak further of the incident. Part of me thinks she just didn't know anything more than the rumor headline herself, but maybe she's just a better non-gossiping Mormon than I'll ever be. Either way, I felt like someone turned off the show just when it started to get good.

In the middle of the complex, there lived a kind family with three teenagers. I'm embarrassed to admit that I thought we were there to help them. I'm humbled to think of all that those parents must have been dealing with, all that must have been weighing on their souls. And yet, a few times they paused to let the sweaty Mormon missionaries come into their home and share their ideas and words. One of their children was a seventeen-year-old girl whom I felt an immediate bond with. Once, I can't remember why, she bought me a gold heart pendant and took it to her pastor to have it blessed. The heart had a cross down the middle, and it broke my heart when my companion expressed that it would be inappropriate for me to wear. Looking back now, I recognize that it probably broke her desperate-to-be-exactly-obedient heart too.

In the same stretch of apartments, there was a young single mom. She had a slew of small children in her care, at least four I was aware of. I called them my baby birds because when we would pass their complex, they would run to me, squealing, dirty bare feet and all. Once at my feet with their sticky hands grasping my skirt, they would throw their heads back with their mouths gaping wide. I would then drip warm water into their mouths from the hose of my CamelBak backpack. The first few times we tried to visit their mom, she wasn't home. When we finally caught her at home, we found out she had been in the hospital recovering from a failed suicide attempt. The mother couldn't have been over twenty-five, but she looked rough and aged. My companions sat on the torn floral sofa that caved in at the center with her and tried to talk her out of prostituting herself to pay for medical bills and food.

I, feeling overwhelmed and completely aware of my inability to help this woman, corralled my wild little baby birds into the corner and sang them Primary songs while showing pictures of Jesus on pass-along cards. I tried to not think about what could happen to my baby birds as they slept on a dirty bare mattress in the room next to their mom's if she let men into their home.

As we began the fifth round of "I am a Child of God," I heard my companion say to the mother, "You have lived quite a journey." At the time, the phrase felt simplistic and ignorantly offensive to the life this woman had been given. But as I look back at my own life thus far, "a journey" feels like the proper way to describe my own path.

For the vast majority of my young life, I defined myself by being a Mormon, and I was dang good at it. The faith and diligence of my parents had given me much. Specifically, my mother taught me by example to seriously study the scriptures daily and attend the temple weekly. I looked for opportunities to keep the commandments of the gospel and the rules of the Church rather than reasons why I was the exception to them.

Though in high school, I often opted for a hotdog and piña colada Slurpee from the 7-Eleven rather than attending my seminary classes, I made up for lost time in my religious studies during my junior and senior year while modeling. When I left for New York for the very first time, my mom gave me a brand-new set of scriptures and the small paper pamphlet of lessons used in the adult Sunday School classes. She instructed me to do a lesson a day, and that's what I did. In the small margins, I would write answers the discussion-prompting questions and cross-references to relate scripture chains of my own.

When I got my mission call in the spring of 2010, I worked to receive my endowment right away. I would enter the MTC early July and I was determined to "understand" and feel comfortable in the temple by the time I left. At this time, I was living in Provo and working four hours each morning as a receptionist of the BYU Employee Benefits Office. After my shift, I would walk to the Provo Utah Temple and sit through an afternoon endowment session. I was attending several sessions a week and felt exactly how I wanted to because of it.

On my mission, I felt more at home than I had ever before. For the first time in my life, I felt like my community valued the skills I had to offer. Having spent much time studying the gospel and living on my own by age twenty-one, I was brave and bold in a way that made me a shiny missionary. My years as a model, working with new adults daily, gave me a cool confidence and charisma that served me as I approached strangers on the street. More than anything, I was confident and comfortable in vocalizing my love for the mission and love for the gospel. I had the gifts that we as Mormons like to rank high on the list of desirable spiritual gifts.

As I look back, I feel sorry for the young men and women who have spiritual gifts that are no less valuable in our Heavenly Parent's eyes but that get put on the backburner by our community and culture. I feel sorry for myself because I know I missed out on learning some great lessons from these missionaries.

After my mission, I did my best to show up for activities, visiting teaching appointments, and Saturday morning building cleanings in my YSA wards. I tried to date men who looked like good, faithful priesthood holders. And I considered myself faithful when I ended relationships when I discovered that they were actually complex humans with stories more complicated than what I thought were supposed to fill the pages of good, faithful priesthood holders' tales.

If twenty-two-year-old Rosie would have found herself in a relationship with the male version of twenty-eight-year-old Rosie, she would have said, "You are a good man, and I know God loves you, but I know this is not the path for me. We 'Mormon' differently. I'm looking for someone with whom I can be 'equally yoked.'"

Imagine my surprise when years of doing my very best to be a good Mormon girl led me to a place of questioning. It was my deep study of President Nelson's talk "A Plea to My Sisters" that made me believe that my feminine voice, my story, my opinions, and my thoughts were of equal value to my male peers in the kingdom of God. It was my belief in "The Family: A Proclamation to the World" that taught me that I, as a woman, am different than males. That I contribute and bring to the table a point of view that men do not because we are different. It was the burning in my heart while I listened to Elder Oaks's "The Keys and Authority of the Priesthood" teach that women serve, teach, and act with Priesthood authority because "what other authority can it be?"[1]

It was all of these good and true things that made sirens go off in my head when only one woman spoke in general conference spring of 2017, which led me to realize the precedence of only two women speaking in the general session of the most important meetings of the Church for decades.

When the Spirit testified to me the truth of Elder Nelson's and Elder Oaks's talks, I believed firmly in the truth of their words. I felt a disconnect between the words and the actions, which led to a slew of questions and doubts.

It is difficult and painful to consider whether the Church that you have sacrificed for and given so much to doesn't truly value you because you are a woman. The Church has always been a beacon in my eyes. A shining light leading the down the path toward good and truth for the rest of the world to follow. The perfect glass box I had put the Church in began to crack when I considered that the Church may be, in some ways, stumbling along the sometimes bright and sometimes dim path right along the rest of us.

In the words of Ashley Mae Hoiland in *One Hundred Birds Taught Me to Fly*: "In the place where absolute surety and comfort once lived, now confusion, bitterness, and sadness surfaced from the depths of my spirit."[2]

First thing Tuesday morning after General Conference Spring 2017, I was in the temple. I dressed in white and headed straight upstairs to a surprisingly crowded celestial room. I drew a handful of Kleenexes from a box on an end table and found an empty chair in a far corner. Hunched over, I began to pray and cry.

I asked my Father in Heaven if I had this all wrong. Maybe I really am less valued because I'm a woman. Maybe my ideas are less important or less needed. As I attempted to play my own devil's advocate, I felt like my chest cavity was filling with hardened cement. As I tried to open mind my to the possibility of simply being wrong about my divine nature, I felt a firm "no." In that moment, I felt a bit of a commotion happening around me. I opened my eyes and through blurred vision noticed I was sitting in the middle of a long line of young men and women standing shoulder to shoulder around the perimeter of the celestial room. Though momentarily confused, I quickly realized that these were missionaries lining up to hug their mission mom and president. I watched at the older man and woman made their way down the line. The President shook each missionary's hand with both of his hands in that sweet old man way. However, before each missionary got a handshake, they got a huge all-encompassing hug from the woman. I began to weep as I watched her throw her arms around and squeeze each elder and sister as though they were her favorite child. Every single missionary looked at her with stars in their eyes, and it was clear they felt a massive amount of love and respect for her and from her.

As I observed this woman wrap the pure love of Christ around each and every one of the missionaries, I felt the distinct presence and importance of my Heavenly Mother. I felt very aware that She was always near. She would always be the first to wrap Her arms around Her children. I learned that She plays an active role in helping us come back to Her. Heavenly Mother isn't taking a break while Her kids are away at school. Heavenly Mother spends Her days and nights serving us. She mourns with us. She comforts us. She encourages us. She strengthens us. She actively plays a crucial role in the plan of salvation. She matters, and because She matters, I, and all of Her daughters, matter.

Though I am still coming to understand our role, I have zero doubt that women are types of our Mother, and it feels deeply and fundamentally wrong to my heart to ignore or diminish our value and our contribution.

As I continued to quietly sob in the celestial room, I wished I could talk to someone I knew. I longed to share these big feelings with someone in hopes of receiving comfort. I knew my aunt and uncle, Carolyn and Rick Evans, were somewhere in the temple at the moment. Rick was a sealer at the Salt Lake Temple on Tuesday mornings, so I knew he would likely be serving in one of the small sealing rooms that lined the hallway just outside the celestial room. I kept my head down as I left the celestial room in an attempt to hide my puffy eyes and blotchy cheeks. The one moment I glanced ahead, I locked eyes with my Aunt Carolyn sitting on a bench outside of the celestial room. I immediately resumed my sobbing and crumpled into her arms.

Through my sobs, I tried to explain to her that my heart ached to hear more women's voices and teachings. I confessed that I believed Elder Nelson's words that it is important for women to lead out and share their voices, but that there seemed to be some kind of disconnect or unspoken boundaries placed on that importance. My Aunt Carolyn, like a true daughter of Heavenly Mother, wrapped her arms around me and let me feel sad. She didn't tell me I was being dramatic. She didn't tell me to consider how often each female leader would have to speak in order to reach a more balanced representation. She didn't try to give any excuse or reason. She validated me and my feelings and that brought me more peace than any valid explanation for the lack of women's voices else could have. Then she said, "I think you should tell him. Elder Nelson is a good man. Maybe write him a kind and calm letter and let him know how you feel."

I was surprised by this answer because it was frankly something I had never considered. I knew that the Handbook discourages members writing general authorities, but the fact that Apostles often share letters from members in their General Conference talks conflicts that standard. I felt comfortable with the idea of reaching out to Elder Nelson because I had briefly interacted with him while working at the Church. Not many months before, I was sitting in Elder Nelson's office filming him talk about the highlights of his ministry for a short film to be played at his ninetieth birthday party.

As I drove home, I decided that I was going to write Elder Nelson an email, but before that, I would write a Facebook post. I was going to follow his council and make my voice heard.

In this Facebook post, I did my best to clarify my love for the gospel of Jesus Christ and my commitment to the Church charged with stewardship of that gospel. I also expressed my reasoning and hope for better representation for the women of the Church.

This is what I wrote:

Only one woman spoke at #ldsconf and this is what I think about it. It's long. You've been warned.

Before we get started, let me introduce myself to any of you who may not know me.

My name is Rosemary Card. I'm 27 and 3/4 years old. I serve in my singles ward in Salt Lake as a Sacrament Meeting Coordinator and am a good not great visiting teacher.

I graduated from BYU, served in the Arizona Mesa Mission, taught at the MTC, interned at The More Good Foundation, worked on the "I'm A Mormon" campaign with Bonneville Communications, shot and produced films for the Church's Publishing Service Department, and own a LDS Temple dress company. While working at the Church I worked on the Bible Videos, My Plan (a new program for missionaries in their last transfer to help them transition to home life), did social Media for Elder Bednar's "Flood the Earth" campaign at BYU Education Week, helped shoot and produce Elder Nelson's 90th birthday video, an interview with Elder Holland about his family history, and a video of President Packer telling the stories behind artifacts in his office. Also, on average I speak to about five young women's groups a month about my time as an international model and how I found happiness through the gospel of Jesus Christ.

The above resume dump is not to brag or to get you to set me up with your brother. (If anything it is a little embarrassing.) I share this to let you know that I'm not just a Mormon. Along with being deeply committed to the Gospel and doctrine of Jesus Christ I live, eat, and breathe Mormon Church culture. You don't get more Mormon than me. However, in full disclosure, I don't have fake ivy in my kitchen so I guess I could up my Mormon game in that area. Nobody's perfect.

As part of my company I run an Instagram account with over 18,000 predominantly LDS female followers. This entails hosting a weekly Talk Club in which we all study the same talk during the week and then share with each other what we learned on Sunday. Recently, I picked "A Plea to My Sisters" by Elder Russel M. Nelson for the Q.NOOR Talk Club to study. I consider this talk, along with Elder Oaks' "The Keys and Authority of the Priesthood," to be some of the most valuable words for the modern Church on women's roles.

I would encourage you to read these talks on your own, but you only really need to go as far as the talk summary underneath the youtube video at www.lds.org/general-conference/2015/10/a-plea-to-my-sisters to understand the main message. It reads, "We need your strength, your conversion, your conviction, your ability to lead, your wisdom, and your voices."

"WE NEED" not "it would be nice for you to share sometimes" or "if there is leftover time we can let you can have a little." Please also note it says "WE" not "Women only."

Elder Nelson's exact words are "We, your brethren, need your strength, your conversion, your conviction, your ability to lead, your wisdom, and your voices. The kingdom of God is not and cannot be complete without women who make sacred covenants and then keep them, women who can speak with the power and authority of God!7" (note: please keep reading for more regarding what authority women of God can speak with.)

I crave the female voice. I crave examples and stories of strong female disciples of Christ. There aren't very many of them included in the scriptures so I devour books like "Daughters in my Kingdom" and "At The Pulpit" in addition to the stories of Esther, Ruth, and scriptural mentions of other faithful women. I also look forward to hearing from my modern day SHEros each General Conference.

I felt a little bummed that both Saturday sessions lacked any of these, according to Elder Nelson, NEEDED voices. But I was sure we would get exactly what we needed in the Sunday sessions. Sunday kicked off with a bang, after sweet words of our President Monson, Sister Joy D. Jones taught powerful doctrine applicable to all members of the Church regardless of gender, marital status or race. I couldn't wait to hear what the next sister would teach us. Every time the next few speakers were announce and I heard "Brother" after "Elder" after "Brother" my heart sank. Eleven minutes and twenty-five seconds was all of this NEEDED voice that we got in the eight hours of General Conference.

I LOVED this General Conference with every fiber of my being (see I speak like a Mormon, too) and I wouldn't take back a single message. I believe the messages were inspired by God and what He wanted us to hear.

So if they are all messages from God, why should we care whether they come from a man or a woman?

To answer this I think we should look at a doctrine we, as a Church, have stood firm by and upheld with a lot of effort over the last few years. Women and men, while equal, are different. As a female Mormon I see and experience things differently than male mormons. I learn, teach, lead and problem solve differently. When we listen and learn from people who are different than us we deepen our pool of knowledge and understanding. Women and men are different. Just as I learn from the male voice, men can and should learn from the female voice.

Female and male speakers in General Conference all share the word of God. However, they are still individuals with unique experiences and understandings that shape the messages they share. A female speaker if different than a male speaker. Just as a female listener is different than a male listener. Given that over 50% of the Church membership is female, I don't think there is any shortage of needed female speakers or listeners. However, there is a shortage of opportunity. I agree with Elder Nelson. The female voice is NEEDED and we all, men and women, miss out when it is lacking.

In D&C 25 the Lords says to Emma Smith "7 And thou shalt be ordained under his hand to expound scriptures, and to exhort the church, according as it shall be given thee by my Spirit." Speaking in conference is not a duty requiring priesthood office. It is a duty requiring priesthood authority, also know as God's authority, which conveniently is available to both men and women. In an address to women President Joseph Feilding Smith said "You can speak with authority, because the Lord has placed authority upon you." In the words of Elder Oaks, "We are not accustomed to speaking of women having the authority of the priesthood in their Church callings, but what other authority can it be?"

In my two years working in the film department of the Church I was blessed to work closely with a few of the apostles. I love these men. I respect them and know they are doing the VERY best they can. I know they respect women and value their contributions.

Gospel doctrine is pure and eternal. It does not change. The Church of Jesus Christ of Latter-day Saints, charged with the dissemination of that Doctrine, does have traditions that can and in some instances should change. Having only men pray in conference was a tradition. A tradition that we changed. As far as I understand, having a predominately male lineup for General Conference is a tradition. A tradition that we can change for the betterment of everyone.

I don't know why there is such a lack of opportunity for men and women to learn from women in General Conference. However, I do know that I will follow the council of The Twelve and do all that I can to make my voice heard. I and women and men like me, will continue to raise our voices and seek progress. If you have any problem with this, I would invite you to take it up with Elder Nelson. :)

Note: Please don't say Women's Conference makes up the lack because men have priesthood and men speak at Women's

Conference, but women don't speak at Priesthood. Additionally, it still shows the lack of opportunity for men to learn from women.

After clicking "post," I was glued to my computer for the next three days. Hundreds of comments poured in. Comments ranged from men and women voicing support to men and women saying I was "tempting God" and that I was one of the people the Book of Mormon talks about who will lead members astray in the last days. Comments came as far as strangers around the world to members of my own extended family. Let's just say there were a LOT of feelings shared on that thread. I felt like it was important that I stay involved in the discussion and did my best to help people understand my intentions, but I learned very quickly that you can't win them all.

Though I did get a number of DMs from people trying to get me to stop, I got many more DMs from people who encouraged me on. The vast majority of DMs came from members who had stepped away from the Church for various reasons. The common theme was "this gives me hope." More or less active members expressed their love, support, and gratitude. Their messages taught me the importance of having tricky conversations and making room for people to share thoughts that may be against the cultural grain of the Church.

When things started quieting down on Facebook, I wrote the following email to Elder Nelson.

Hi Elder Nelson!

My name is Rosemary Card. You may not remember me (which I don't blame you for) but I helped film your 90th birthday video. Please see attached photo.

I have stopped working for the Church because I launched a company designing and selling temple dresses that are designed to help more young women feel more at home in the House of the Lord. (qnoor.com). This little company has an Instagram account with over 18,000 followers. The Q.NOOR community and I have been doing a talk club where every week we study a specific talk on our own and then share what we learned in on a common post on the following Sunday.

Recently we studied, "A Plea to My Sisters" and "The Keys and Authority of the Priesthood" by Elder Oaks. I LOVE these talks. They have truly inspired me and given me so much hope. I have listened to them over and over.

I am deeply committed to the gospel of Jesus Christ. I love this gospel more than anything because it truly brings me joy. I hope you can truly feel that in my words.

When I watched general conference this weekend I felt uplifted and inspired in every way. I wouldn't take back a single message. I have no doubt they were inspired by God. At the same time, I felt a true sadness that I wasn't able to gain those same powerful messages from a few more women.

The gospel teaches that gender matters. It influences who we are, how we teach, how we learn, and how we experience this life. I felt so validated and encouraged by your talk when you said that "WE NEED your voices."

Elder Nelson, I ache for more of these voices. I devour the words in Women's Conference but I wish, maybe selfishly, for more women's voice in the general sessions so men and women can benefit from them. I know I can learn from men's voices. I do so every conference, Sunday, and day when I read my scriptures. But our voices are different and "in a happy way."

I know I am preaching to the choir, and I don't want to seem like I am instructing you. This is truly meant in the most humble and teachable voice. I'm just wondering if you could share a little bit of light with me as to the lack of women's voice in the general sessions. I'm sorry to take up so much of your time and to ask for more. I know you are incredibly busy with much more important things.

I recently posted my feeling about this on Facebook. There are currently almost 600 comments. Many of them calling me apostate and condemning me. I know they are good people and it is all just a misunderstanding. Not sure why I feel the need to disclaim that, but there you have it.

Thank you for your lifetime of service and all that you have done to personally bless my life.

Love,
Rosie

Attached to the email was a photo of me lint-rolling his suit coat before we began filming. I didn't know Elder Nelson's email, but having worked at the Church, I knew most emails within the organization followed a standard format. I made four of my best educated guesses of what his email may be and then sent it off to all four of them. One email address immediately bounced back. Within the next day or two I got emails back from two church employees that said, "This isn't Elder Nelson's email address." I assumed the same was true for the fourth email address and I moved on. I had done my best.

The next week I got the following letter from Elder Nelson.

Dear Rosemary,

Thank you for your thoughtful email. It made me happy to know that the recent general conference was meaningful to you. Also, thank you for sharing your insights and concerns. They are very much appreciated.

We love, appreciate, and recognize the worth of every sister. Each has an incredible and divine capacity to be an influence for good in the home, Church, community, and world. We were especially grateful to learn from several sister auxiliary leaders in the first session of general conference. Their messages were marvelous and did much to encourage, uplift, and inspire our Father in Heaven's Children.

Rosemary, your great faith and loyal devotion to the Lord Jesus Christ and His church are evident and very much appreciated. You and many others have been blessed and will continue to benefit from the service and love that you willingly give.

May our Heavenly Father's choicest blessings continue to be with you in all that you do. Please accept by best wishes always.

Most cordially,
Signed Russel M. Nelson

Besides, just being super cool to receive a personal letter from a member of the Twelve, this letter was important to me for two reasons. One: He acknowledged and thanked me for sharing my voice. Two: He didn't solve my problem.

Elder Nelson's letter was kind and good and it also left space me for to figure this out for myself.

While working at the Church, I was part of a small team assigned to handle the social media for Elder Bednar's #floodtheearth talk at BYU Education Week. The day before his big talk, I drove down to Provo to get a few behind-the-scenes shots of Elder Bednar practicing in the empty Marriot Center. While he practiced, I wove through the empty rows of stadium seats snapping photos of him.

Once he was finished, he stepped off the stage and began speaking to a group of men who looked like high-up Church employees. I continued to quietly capture a few photos of him and the group. Suddenly, Elder Bednar stepped away from the group and approached me. Thinking I was about to get in trouble, my stomach sank, and I immediately blurted out, "I'm sorry. I'm not taking these pictures for my social media. I work for the Church."

He smiled and said, "Actually, I was wondering if you could give me some feedback on my talk. Was there anything you didn't understand? Anything that made you clutch?" I'm not sure whose eyes were bigger, mine or the men in suits Elder Bednar was just talking to. I tripped over my words for a few seconds and then got out, "To be honest, I wasn't really listening. I was focused on getting the shots we need." Looking a little disappointed he politely smiled and began to turn back to the group. Trying to recover I said, "But I read it on Sunday. They sent it out for us to prepare ahead of time. It was really good. I remember there was something about the beginning of the talk that I didn't really understand how it connected to the rest of it, but I can't remember any specifics. I know that's not super helpful to you, but that it just what I remember." I didn't include the fact that I read his talk during Sacrament meeting because I was bored.

I distinctly remember the look on the group of men's faces. They were in complete shock that I had just offered somewhat of a critique of an Apostle's talk. I, too, was a little bewildered by my answer, but it was the truth! I sure as heck wasn't going to lie to an Apostle just to butter him up. My head was still trying to process what had just happened a few minutes later when Elder Bednar approached me again. "I know what made you clutch. You didn't understand what my introduction about the apostasy had to do with my message about using social media for missionary work."

I was both shocked and not surprised, and he was totally right. "Yeah, that was it."

"Well I'm not going to explain it to you, because you need to go back and study that for yourself. You need to receive your own inspiration." Then he turned and walked away. My very first thought was, *I just got Elder Bednar'd by Elder Bednar.*

These two experiences are like steel beams reinforcing the foundation of my testimony of personal revelation. Prophets and Apostles and the revelation they can and do receive for the Church are massive blessings of the Restoration. They lead us and guide us and help us in our personal and collective journey back to God. However, we cannot place our personal responsibility to connect with our Heavenly Parents on our Ecclesiastical leaders' shoulders. They are humans, and that isn't their job.

Sometimes I worry that we too often turn to another human with a high calling to tell us what is and isn't okay and rather than putting in the work to ask God ourselves and be accountable to the answer. Our Heavenly Parents and Savior know us on an intimate and unique level. In the inspired words of Cheiko Okasaki:

> Well, my dear sisters, the gospel is the good news that can free us from guilt. We know that Jesus experienced the totality of mortal existence in Gethsemane. It's our faith that he experienced everything- absolutely everything. Sometimes we don't think through the implications of that belief. We talk in great generalities about the sins of all humankind, about the suffering of the entire human family. But we don't experience pain in generalities. We experience it individually. That means he knows what it felt like when your mother died of cancer- how it was for your mother, how it still is for you. He knows what it felt like to lose the student body election. He knows that moment when the brakes locked and the car started to skid. He experienced the slave ship sailing from Ghana toward Virginia. He experienced the gas chambers at Dachau. He experienced Napalm in Vietnam. He knows about drug addiction and alcoholism.
>
> Let me go further. There is nothing you have experienced as a woman that he does not also know and recognize. On a profound level, he understands the hunger to hold your baby that sustains you through pregnancy. He understands both the

physical pain of giving birth and the immense joy. He knows about PMS and cramps and menopause. He understands about rape and infertility and abortion. His last recorded words to his disciples were, "And, lo, I am with you always, even unto the end of the world." (Matthew 28:20) He understands your mother-pain when your five-year-old leaves for kindergarten, when a bully picks on your fifth-grader, when your daughter calls to say that the new baby has Down syndrome. He knows your mother-rage when a trusted babysitter sexually abuses your two-year-old, when someone gives your thirteen-year-old drugs, when someone seduces your seventeen-year-old. He knows the pain you live with when you come home to a quiet apartment where the only children are visitors, when you hear that your former husband and his new wife were sealed in the temple last week, when your fiftieth wedding anniversary rolls around and your husband has been dead for two years. He knows all that. He's been there. He's been lower than all that. He's not waiting for us to be perfect. Perfect people don't need a Savior. He came to save his people in their imperfections. He is the Lord of the living, and the living make mistakes. He's not embarrassed by us, angry at us, or shocked. He wants us in our brokenness, in our unhappiness, in our guilt and our grief.

You know that people who live above a certain latitude and experience very long winter nights can become depressed and even suicidal, because something in our bodies requires whole spectrum light for a certain number of hours a day. Our spiritual requirement for light is just as desperate and as deep as our physical need for light. Jesus is the light of the world. We know that this world is a dark place sometimes, but we need not walk in darkness. The people who sit in darkness have seen a great light, and the people who walk in darkness can have a bright companion. We need him, and He is ready to come to us, if we'll open the door and let him.[3]

Our leaders are inspired and we should be, too. And so, began my journey in the world.

In my attempt to navigate this foreign spiritual landscape, I tried to draw parallels with other stories of people who doubted. I realized that I had always assumed that people placed themselves in these situations through sin. However, as much as I tried, I couldn't convince myself that I had committed a sin grievous enough to justify what I consider abandonment of the Spirit. Over and over, a phrase I had heard from Elder Bednar came into my head. "Do your best to be a good girl." That is exactly what I had done. Were there men and women out there who were more righteous than me? Most definitely—there are thousands upon thousands. But if Elder Holland can say no young man loved his mission more than he did, I give myself permission to hyperbolically say no woman tried harder to be a good girl than I did.

Because I knew how hard I tried, I had to give place to the idea that maybe, I was exactly where God wanted me to be. Maybe this wasn't a wasteland that I had fallen from the path into. Maybe this was the place the path of my early twenties led to.

> I think we all feel some tension between our religious convictions and the secular times in which we live. In one way or another, modernism invades and unsettles our thinking, perhaps our thinking about our fields, perhaps our personal beliefs. What I hope we all realize is that this tension is not to be suppressed or regretted. Unanswerable as some questions are, we need not lament the discomfort they bring. The strain of believing in unbelieving times, is not a handicap or a burden. It is a stimulus and a prod. It is precisely out of such strains that creative work issues forth. And we can take satisfaction in knowing that we are in this together.
>
> —Richard Lyman Bushman[4]

🕊 On my mission, there was a week when I felt absolutely nothing. I remember standing on a hot corner in Scottsdale watching the sweat drip down my shins and pool in my clunky Dansko MaryJane clogs while my companion tried to intercept a man jogging with his dog a few paces ahead. I felt like an empty shell, and I couldn't bring myself to testify of something that I didn't feel burning in me. As I look back, I recognize the immaturity in my expectations of the Spirit, but I don't blame young Sister Card. Between those tearful girls' camp testimony meetings and MTC devotionals, I grew to believe that the Spirit made His presence known much like a high schooler desperate for attention. When the Spirit enters the room, the Spirit made sure everyone knows it.

My sweet angel of a companion felt uneasy around my lack of participation and recommended I meet with our mission president, whose office was nearby. As I sat in the office of President Spencer Ellsworth, a human who I will always love more than most, I explained, ashamed, that I didn't feel *anything*, let alone the Spirit. He essentially asked if I had been a good obedient girl, which I confirmed. He then said that sometimes the Spirit may feel distant because we have sinned, and sometimes, like a parent sliding their fingers from the clammy palms of a child learning to walk, the Spirit may feel distant because we need to take steps on our own. He essentially asked me to consider whether my commitment to the gospel was conditional on a life of a never-ending thread of flashy spiritual experiences; "I will go, I will do!" moments of bravery and surprise anonymous checks under your door when you pick tithing over Christmas gifts. [Or am I willing to stay even when it is uncomfortable? Am I willing to stay through months of leaving three-hour church blocks feeling the same as when I entered? Am I willing to stay when life as a Mormon feels like a day-to-day routine rather than a shiny battle victory?]

> [But] as for me, the silence and the emptiness is so great, that I look and do not see—Listen and do not hear—the tongue moves [in prayer] but does not speak . . . I want you to pray for me— that I let Him have [a] free hand.
>
> —Mother Teresa[5]

As I sat in that purple-and-blue floral cushioned seat, I couldn't imagine that one day I would also be asking myself, "Am I willing to stay when I feel like Church policy is being more harmful than helpful? Am I willing to stay when I feel wrongly less than because I was created in the image of the feminine half of the divine couple we call 'God'?"

My oldest sister, Sam, taught me how to ride my bike without training wheels. We lived on Cliff Swallow Drive in Sandy, Utah, and a full-sized candy bar was the promised prize if I accomplished the task. Sam, only four-ish years my senior, would hold on to the back of my seat and run alongside my bike, steadying me as I hesitantly pedaled. Anyone who has learned to ride a bike knows how scary those first moments are when you feel that steadying hand release its grip from the back of your seat. Anyone who kept pedaling also knows the thrill and excitement that comes when you realize you can continue without it.

I in no way am trying to say that we don't need the Spirit's guidance in our lives or that we can do this on our own. However, I am saying that I believe our Heavenly Parents want us to be profitable servants who act, rather than unprofitable servants who wait around to be acted upon.

In some very real aspects, I am still in the "panicked to be pedaling on my own" phase. My prayers often resemble my younger self screaming to my sister Sam to no let go. "I'm not ready! I'm going to crash!!!" I hesitate to say this because I fear discrediting myself by acknowledging that I am less than all-knowing. But the truth is, the best-intentioned imperfect human interpretations of heavenly truths are the best we have, guys.

As time passes, I have grown less panicky and more accepting of this part of my life. When I lost my ability to find the Spirit in some of our favorite rendezvous points, I started looking for the quiet peace in new places. And I found Him. Sometimes in predictable places. Alma 30:44, "All things denote there is a God," rings true to my heart in a way it never had before.

One of my favorite parts of this discovering process was realizing that our Heavenly Parents are reaching out to all of Their children. People all over the world are learning eternal truths. They may call it something different, but no matter what you call it, the gospel is the same. In the words of Elsie Talmage Brandley, "To know the fundamental truths of the gospel is to leave one free to go far and wide, anchored by that knowledge, in search of all else that earth and sea and skies have to teach."[6]

Richard Rohr, a Catholic priest, taught me in his book *Falling Upward* that all eternal progression of any significance into a deeper, more purposeful life comes after a fall. Adam and Eve were not able to begin their process, and our process, of growing and preparing to return home until the Fall. Christ had to die to be resurrected. We must be buried in the water to be reborn.

The late Beverly Campbell's *Eve and the Choice Made in Eden* taught me to love and respect Eve's choice to fall long ago while I was on a study abroad in Jerusalem. Before I left for the most amazing four months in the Holy Land, I knew I would be spending much of my time learning more about Jesus Christ and His life. I decided that since so much of my school studies would be focused on the man who enables me to progress after this life and return to God, I wanted to spend my personal studies learning about the woman who enabled me to even begin the journey. If Nephi taught us that it's necessary and good to sometimes do things differently than the standard rules, Eve is the OG of this principle. What Eve did took serious guts, and we all owe our lives to her. I'll be interested to learn from her how much she understood about what her choice to eat the fruit entailed. Maybe she knew she was turning the key that would enable the entire plan of salvation to light up, but maybe she was just testing out a feeling within her own spiritual experiment.

In *At the Pulpit* is one of the most relevant and important talks of our time, and as far as this book is concerned, I'm the expert on this, so don't doubt me. Elsie Mae Brandley, who I quoted just prior, gave the talk "The Religious Crisis of Today" in 1934, but she must have been a true wizard, because I'm convinced she meant it for us in the 2000s. I deserve a medal for the restraint and respect for copyright laws I practiced by not just copying and pasting the whole talk right here into this book. I'm going to give you sweet tastes, but you've got to go search out and devour the whole thing if you really want to enjoy it.

Elsie quotes Glenn Frank in "The Will to Doubt":

The will to believe has given us our great saints; the will to doubt has given us our greatest scientists. The goal of the intelligent [woman] is a character in which the will to believe of the saint and the will to doubt of the scientist meet and mingle. Neither alone makes a whole [woman]. A merely blind faith gives us a soft saint; a merely blind doubt gives us a hard scientist. Humanity owes much to the saint and much to the scientist, but humanity would fare badly if the world were people solely by saints with a blind faith or by scientists with a blind doubt. Modern science is modest. It suspends judgement when it does not know. In all other fields—religion, politics, and so on—we must learn to do likewise. We must act in the light of the best we know at any given moment, but we must be willing to hold our beliefs open to revision in the light of new facts. Thus we can combine saint and scientist.[7]

Elsie teaches acceptance of the open acknowledgment of our limited understanding and encourages all to seek to refine and improve our understanding. Wisely, she follows up with, "Fruit is eaten without knowing botany; stars are loved in ignorance of astronomy; telegrams are sent with no knowledge of the Morse code [or modern-day coding]; love and friendship, home and books and nature become dear and of great value with little attempt to explain technical reasons."[8] We can and should still expect, strive, and allow ourselves to feel peace from the gospel of Jesus Christ regardless of how many experiments of faith and doubt currently operate in our lives. If there is one burned-out lightbulb in your house, you can still live a happy and illuminated life in the light of the others. Can you imagine walking away from your home and searching for a new one just because a few bulbs burned out? If you can, you're really weird and I want to know where you live so I can finders keepers it at some point. If you can't imagine giving up your home that you likely worked very hard for and have really enjoyed just because of a few dim areas, maybe you should think twice before parting with your spiritual home for the same reasons.

We have all heard, plenty of times, the teaching to not be "cafeteria Mormons." The meaning behind this idea is to encourage members to completely embrace the doctrine, principles, and culture of our faith. I get it. On many levels, I agree with the idea of it. However, if you can't presently stomach the meatloaf, but can handle the peas and pudding, fill up your tray with what you can, and come sit with us! There is plenty of room at the Savior's table. No matter what you choose to leave off your tray for the time being, the Savior has a seat next to Him saved for you. Chances are He will try to get you to try just a tiny taste of His sandwich, but His friendship is not conditional upon your plate being a perfect match to His. He is just glad you're there.

One of the most validating passages of scripture at this point in my life is Alma 32:35–36:

After you have tasted this light is your knowledge perfect?

> Behold I say unto you, Nay; neither must you lay aside your faith, for ye have only exercised your faith to plant the seed that ye might try the experiment to know if the seed was good.

Faith is believing in things that are not seen . . . or even just seen dimly. By this definition, as much as some people on the internet or within my extended family might disagree, this is the most faithful time in my life. Never before have I knowingly relied on my Savior so fully. Never before have I ached so deeply to see His hand in the world around me.

In my early teen years, I would spend a few weeks each summer with the Bennion family in Spring City, Utah. In my city-girl eyes, Joe and Lee were magical creatures living off the land and working jobs that were more about caring for their hearts than they were about climbing the corporate ladder. Joe is a fine art potter who failed his first college pottery class. His shop, Horseshoe Mountain Pottery, is open 24/7. Travelers are able to pick pieces and leave their money in a cashbox built into an interior door that separates the storefront from the studio. Lee, also a fine artist, paints women, children, and animals that make you feel more than you see.

Their artisan home—complete with a large yard, garden, stable, and chicken coop—was magic to me. I spent summer days painting fences, playing with the dogs, grooming horses, and avoiding the chickens like the feathered cannibalistic dinosaurs they are. Lee would often take me up into the Horseshoe Mountains for long trail rides, Lee on Tiki and I on Blue.

Inside their home, on the main level is the guest bathroom/laundry room. The inside of the door is covered with bumper stickers. For some reason, one sticker always stuck out to me. *QUESTIONS ARE GOOD* in big bold letters on a contrasting background. I read that sticker over and over. At that point in my life, I didn't have lots of questions. Joseph Smith was a true prophet with great hair and spent his days racing kids through green fields. I knew the Church was true and it never made mistakes. And that pretty much summed up my testimony.

In one of my favorite books, *A Story Like the Wind*, the main character, a young boy named Francois growing up in the Bush of colonial Africa, discovers a whimsical man of an ancient African tribe, Xhabbo, who was wounded on his journey to the ancestral land of his people.

The man was on a map-less journey to a place he had never been. He spoke of following a "tapping" in his heart. Something both very real and indescribable was directing him to his family's holy place.

> It is not the beating of the heart. It is utterly different. It is like a finger tapping against the skin of the chest, like a finger on a drum, telling the ear to listen and hear talk of things from a far-off place. All we Bushmen are taught from the time we are young that we have to expect this tapping inside ourselves in order to know things that eyes cannot see, the ears cannot hear and the nose . . . cannot smell.[9]

For me, reading that bumper sticker *QUESTIONS ARE GOOD* was like a tapping in my heart. Something about it felt true to the core and almost like a mantra to me. Little tween me may not have had a lot of questions, but I knew they were good.

As I have grown older, this mantra, still holding place in my soul, has encouraged me and sustained me. Often in my journey, I have met resistance from those who are uncomfortable with my questions. It doesn't make sense to them how I can consider myself completely committed to the gospel while simultaneously questioning why we do the things we do or believe the things we believe. To some, questions are a scary thing. For good reason! I understand how it can be seen to be safer and easier to not lean into questions. Early on in the important book *Women at Church*, Neylan McBaine shines light on one of the many reasons why Mormons may find discomfort in questions or differing opinions and applications.

> Our highly personal daily faith practices sometimes prompts us to feel overly protective of the way we practice faith. We feel an ownership and spiritual connection to the way we practice our faith, and we feel threatened when others practice differently, as if a different practice devalues what works for us individually. . . . For part of the twentieth century, some sincerely believed that "when the prophet speaks, the thinking is done"— even though George Albert Smith south to dispel this belief after the phrase had become popular, writing, "Even to imply that members of the Church are not to do their own thinking is grossly to misrepresent the true ideal of the Church."[10]

⌈Though asking questions may be uncomfortable, if you don't ask, you may waste time or miss out on personal tutoring.

Honestly, I don't really understand how anyone gets anywhere without questions. Questions lead to searching, and searching often leads to answers. But not always. Sometimes searching just leads to more paths. Questions are more about movement and development than they are about arrival at a destination.⌋

Considering we are a church whose roots go back to a young man asking a question, the practice of seeking more knowledge should be one that makes us excited rather than nervous.

Maybe I'm just starting to notice this theme because it directly applies to my life, but part of me feels that this acceptance and embrace of questions is popping up more and more. Sheri Dew, the woman, the myth, the legend, gave a BYU–I devotional entitled ⌈"Will You Engage in the Wrestle?" a couple of years ago in which she acknowledges that everyone has questions. "Some [questions] are doctrinal, historical, or procedural. Some are intensely personal. . . . Questions are not just good, they are vital, because the ensuing spiritual wrestle leads to answers, to knowledge, and to revelation. And it also leads to greater faith." And then she asks, "Are you willing to engage in the wrestle? In an ongoing spiritual wrestle?"[11] ⌋The wrestle she nods to is described by Enos as the "wrestle which [he] had before God, before [he received] a remission of [his] sins" (Enos 1:2) and by Alma when he "wrestl[ed] with God in mighty prayer" (Alma 8:10).⌋

In 2017, I took a meditation course from Thomas Wirthlin McConkie—with a name like that, you know he is legit. In one of our meetings focused on conflict, Thomas made the point that most of us are only willing to really hash out disagreements with people we deeply love, trust, and respect. This made me think of when I was a teen and I had saved up for ballet lessons. Early on, I had felt like my teacher was constantly picking on me. She was always pointing out what I was doing wrong over everyone else. When I fussed about it, she said, "I'll stop correcting you when I stop believing in you." I have come to feel empowered by the understanding that it is my deep love for this faith and Church that motivates me to ask questions. If I didn't care about the Church, I can promise you that I wouldn't be investing this much time, heart, and effort into my questions and faith.

Many, if not the vast majority, of my peers have engaged in wrestling with questions or are currently mid awkward wrestling outfit. Everyone's wrestle is their own, and I don't pretend to know anyone else's particular experience. I can only speak for myself. And in myself, I have observed a tendency to "half-ask." Yes, I am comfortable enough to ask questions and begin researching through history and documents to find my answers. But am I willing to fully ask God? Am I willing to accept an answer from my Heavenly Parents that can't be found in documents and articles? Am I willing to accept the difficult "no answer" answer?

In the words of my dear friend Lee Hale, "It's okay to not ask, but if you do ask, you better be willing to go all the way because when you ask you get hit with doubt first and then you have to push through to the truth." In many cases, this truth is only given to those willing to ask and work for it.

"The object of prayer is not to change the will of God but to secure for ourselves and for others blessings that God is already willing to grant but that are made conditional on our asking for them" (Bible Dictionary, "Prayer").

For me, though it takes a heck of a lot of faith at times, I have found that God is the best primary source. God is able to give knowledge that can't be found on the internet. Our Heavenly Parents are able to give peace when things just don't seem to line up.

We are all familiar with Alma's teaching of experimenting with a seed of faith. Though I hesitate to tell someone how to interpret or apply scripture in their life, I think it is important to consider that the seed that Alma encourages us to test out is the love of God. This seed is perfect and it is good. Luckily for many of us, it's also pretty hard to screw up. When fruits of individuals or institutions taste less than good to me, I can always fall back on the sweet and delicious fruit of the love of God. It is always oh so good.

This book is simply my story. It is flawed, and considering I'm only in my late twenties, this story is far from complete (fingers crossed). But, incredibly, just like yours, it matters. Be happy, strong, and kind and follow the tapping.

Notes

1. Dallin H. Oaks, "The Keys and Authority of the Priesthood," *Ensign*, May 2014.

2. Ashley Mae Hoiland, *One Hundred Birds Taught Me to Fly: The Art of Seeking God* (Provo, Utah: Neal A. Maxwell Institute, 2016), 86.

3. Chieko N. Okazaki, *Lighten Up* (Salt Lake City: Deseret Book, 1993), 174.

4. Richard L. Bushman in *To Be Learned Is Good: Essays on Faith and Scholarship in Honor of Richard Lyman Bushman* (Provo, Utah: Neal A. Maxwell Institute, 2018).

5. Mother Teresa as quoted in David Van Biema, "Mother Teresa's Crisis of Faith," *TIME*, August 23, 2007, http://time.com/4126238/mother-teresas -crisis-of-faith.

6. Elsie Talmage Brandley in *The Improvement Era*, August 1934.

7. Glenn Frank, as quoted in Elsie Talmage Brandley, "The Religious Crisis of Today," Mutual Improvement Association June Conference Assembly Hall, Temple Square, Salt Lake City, June 9, 1934, https://www .churchhistorianspress.org/at-the-pulpit/part-3/32-the-religious-crisis-of -today-elsie-talmage-brandley.

8. Brandley, "The Religious Crisis of Today."

9. Laurens van der Post, *A Story Like the Wind* (New York: William Morrow, 1972), 112.

10. Neylan McBaine, *Women at Church: Magnifying LDS Women's Local Impact* (Draper, UT: Greg Kofford Books, 2014) , 11.

11. Sheri Dew, "Will You Engage in the Wrestle?" (Brigham Young University– Idaho devotional, May 17, 2016), http://www.byui.edu/devotionals /sheri-dew.

Acknowledgments

Many people have played vital roles in helping this book and its stories come about. To those people, thank you.

However, I'm going to save this special place for my parents, Michael J. Card and Liesa R. Card.

Thank you for your endless love and patience. My life has been deeply blessed because of your righteousness, hard work, and sacrifices. Thank you for doing what you felt was right even when it seemed crazy. Thank you. I love you to the moon and back.

About the Author

Rosemary Card is the CEO and founder of Q.NOOR. She has spent the last ten years speaking to groups of women of all ages about her experiences as an international high-fashion runway and print model. Rosemary is a vocal advocate of women's rights and is driven to help women recognize their personal power and responsibility as leaders and agents of positive change through education and self-development. Rosemary lives in Salt Lake City with her goldendoodle, Ted, and is a proud pioneer of the stay-at-home YSA lifestyle. She loves eating at Arby's, watching dog videos on the internet, and playing really poor golf.

Scan to visit

QNOOR.com

 @qnoor_templedress & @rosiecard